The Rules Of The Game

How to "Write Your Own Ticket" in

COLLEGE & BEYOND

W9-BAH-367

Delatorro L. McNeal II

America's #1 Success Coach for College Students & Staff

Foreword by **Professor Joe Martin**
One of America's Top Motivational Professors

The Rules of the Game:
How to "Write You Own Ticket" In College and Beyond!

A Noval Idea Publishing, Inc.

A subsidiary of A Noval Idea, Inc.
P.O. Box 27242
Tampa, FL. 33623

ISBN: 0-9721324-7-1

Cover Design: Melanie Steen
Page Design & Typography: Melanie Steen
Editing: Kahlila G. Mack
Photography: Jerrard Mack

PRINTED IN THE UNITED STATES OF AMERICA
The 3rd Publishing with A Noval Idea, Inc : March 2004

ATTENTION COLLEGE COORDINATORS:
GET THIS BOOK FOR ALL YOUR INCOMING FRESHMAN, STUDENT LEADERS, TRANSFER STUDENTS, AND GRADUATING STUDENTS.
This book is available at quantity discounts for bulk purchases. For additional information regarding A Noval Idea, Inc. visit us on the web at **www.delmcneal.com** or email us at **info@delmcneal.com**, or call us at **1-866-472-8637.**

Other Empowering Products By Delatorro L. McNeal, II Include:

Robbing the Grave of Its Greatness
8 Steps to Birthing Your Best Right Now
Foreword by Drs. Randy & Paula White
The Book

Robbing the Grave of It's Greatness
8 Steps to Birthing Your Best Right Now
The Audio CD Series

How to Achieve Unlimited Success
Strategies for Creating Extraordinary Results
The Book

From a Hunger to a Craving LIVE Video!
Featuring Les Brown

101 Gems of Greatness
Foreword by Les Brown
The Book

101 Gems of Greatness
The Audio CD

Keys to Unlocking Your Greatness
Introduction by Willie Jolley

Better Your Best
LIVE Double CD Series

This book is dedicated in loving memory of
my Great Aunt

Sis. Ardellia Ball Bell Wilder – October 1, 1998

Aunt Dee Dee, thank you for being committed to education as a Head Start Teacher & Aid for 26 years. Ironically, this book is being published while I am at the age of 26, which means that you began your quest to educate others during the same year that I was born. WOW! I honor your dedication, commitment, love, support, and long suffering to mold and shape the hearts and minds of young people. You are in my heart always. I dedicate the impact of this book back to you!

I would also like to dedicate this book to my beautiful and loving wife, Nova T. McNeal. Thanks for ALWAYS encouraging me to encourage others. Thanks for all the nights you sleep alone and allow other colleges and universities to "borrow me for the day". Thanks for traveling with me across the country and motivating me with your smile, your laughter, your support, and your love. You are indeed my heaven sent angel, and I thank you for always pushing me to push others!

In addition, I would like to dedicate this book to my mother – Olivia B. Fatherly who sacrificed a portion of her graduate education in college, in order to raise my older brother Mike and myself. She traded in her books for big-wheels, and she traded in her Danford Fellow Ph.D Scholarship for 2 sons who would one day change the world. She traded making herself a "big name" so that we might be a "big name" one day. Well mom, Thank You for sacrificing back then, so that we can be who we are now!

Finally, I would like to dedicate this book to one of the greatest champions God ever created. My older brother, Michael T. McNeal. You have beaten everything that life has thrown your way. You have overcome life-threatening surgery, and kept a smile on your face and heart the entire time. You have been one of my greatest sources of motivation. Thanks for "giving me a head start!" Also, thanks for doing the "local college thing", so that I could do the "away from home college thing". You are indeed the best brother I could ever ask for. Look out world, MTM Capital Funding Group is coming your way!

Foreword

As an award-winning speaker, author, and professor, I've been blessed with the opportunity to travel the country and speak to more than 450 colleges, universities, and faculty/staff conferences over the past six years. As an educational consultant, I have studied the college and university system from the inside out. One of the things that I have observed is that **many students simply decide to go TO college, while a select few intentionally decide to go THROUGH college.**

In other words, most students work hard just to get TO college, acting as if college is the final destination. I find that students with this type of mindset take much longer to graduate and end up in a financial hospital of massive student loan and credit card debt. Why? Because they thought about college, but they did not think BEYOND! Consequently, **I find that students who have the mindset to go THROUGH college, end up being "Students On A Mission."** They have a purpose! They have a WHY in life.

As I teach in my book **Tricks of the Grade…Street-Smart Strategies for Acing College,** it is vitally important that you have a strong WHY in your life. Why do you want to experience and master college? Why do you want to major in what you are majoring in? Why do you want to make a difference with your career? **The answers to these questions give you STAYING POWER in college while simultaneously giving you the fuel and energy to vision beyond college and into your ultimate destiny in life.** Be the type of student who looks at college as a powerful and purposeful part of your journey to success, and not as the final destination.

One of greatest opportunities that a college student can have is to be **coached to greatness by someone who has "been there and done that."** Delatorro McNeal, II is indeed a Success Coach to college students and staff. In this powerful, paradigm-shifting, and life-changing book, Delatorro, having mastered college, corporate, and academia, now takes a powerful look back over his college experience and leaves behind some of the most powerful nuggets of success (in the form of The Rules of the Game) that I have read in years. He gives you insight, I believe, every incoming, existing, and outgoing college student needs to know and apply.

In this book, *The Rules of the Game: How to Write Your Own Ticket in College and Beyond,* Delatorro masterfully teaches empowerment and success principles that simply are not found in most textbooks. **He educates, equips, and empowers the ordinary student to create and maintain extraordinary results. This book is a GOLDMINE!** Delatorro speaks directly from his heart, his experience, and his wisdom, and **literally shaves YEARS off the learning curve for students.** In my opinion, this book should be required reading in schools all across the country, and I know that it will be.

You know college an the incubator and a catalyst from which your academic, personal, professional, and intellectual greatness is birthed. You are a blessed young adult who is embarking upon a wonderful journey of discovery while in college. **This book will challenge you to take charge of your collegiate experience** and take your destiny into your own hands. Allow me to leave one final challenge with you…
DON'T JUST READ THIS BOOK…LIVE IT!

And in so doing, you will indeed be able to "Write Your Own Ticket…In College & Beyond!"

Prof. Joe Martin Jr., Ed.D.
"America's Top Motivational Professor"
Author of the Top-selling, "Tricks of the Grade"
www.RWuniversity.com

Table of Contents

Author Foreword: Let's Get Clear about Your Wants

I know many of the things that you want. I know you want to:

- **Make** something great of yourself
- **Impact** this world with your gifts and talents
- **Be** significant and successful
- **Fit** into a club, organization, or association
- **Spread** your wings and fly your own course
- **Outdo** your parents and surpass expectations
- **Blaze** a success trail for your younger siblings
- **Be** a positive statistic instead of a negative one
- **Get** a little wild and crazy, now that you can
- **Meet** new people and experience new cultures
- **Be** heard and have your opinion change policy
- **Surround** yourself with positive & uplifting people

I know many of the things that you want. I know you want to:

- **Count** for something & impact your campus
- **Dare** to be different and have people accept you
- **Overcome** your failures and still be successful
- **Develop** meaningful relationships with faculty and staff
- **Master** college financially instead of it mastering you
- **Apply** the knowledge you are gaining in profitable ways
- **Touch** people's lives and encourage others to keep going
- **Develop** a relationship with your higher power
- **Volunteer** your time to learn from those who you admire
- **See** the hours of study, practice, and note-taking pay off
- **Be** well-known, well-respected, and well-admired
- **Not move** in with mom and dad after college
- **Not drown** in student-loan debt after graduation
- **Succeed** and build the dream life you so much deserve

It is my sincere hope, prayer, dream, and expectation that this book will empower to you achieve all of this and more. Get your pen, your highlighter, and **LET'S GET STARTED!**

Chapter 1

Classroom & Academic Success

Rule #1

Become more than a Student and More than a Number!

Determine within your mind and heart that you - as an empowered young adult represent far more than just a name on a roster and an 8-digit number that was assigned to you at birth. So many times, especially in college - faculty, staff, administration, and financial aid services request from you either your name or social security number. Being addressed by these two types of identification can condition you to feeling as though what you are called by, or looked up as in the database is, in fact, who you are. I DON'T THINK SO!

You are more than a student. **You are a world changer!**
You are more than a student. **You are a lifesaver!**
You are more than a student. **You are a survivor!**
You are more than a student. **You are a blessed original!**
You are more than a student. **You are an academic success!**
You are more than a student. **You are a potential millionaire!**

You, my friend, are much more than a book-bag-toting, car-wanting, major-changing, club-going young adult who is attending college just to have something to do. NO…

You are more than a number. **You are a future entrepreneur.**
You are more than a number. **You are the CEO of your life.**
You are more than a number. **You are a purposed person.**
You are more than a number. **You are a blossoming A student.**
You are more than a number. **You are a future mom or dad.**
You are more than a number. **You are a leader and a problem solver.**

Classroom & Academic Success

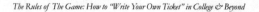

My friend, **NEVER allow your circumstances to dictate your identity. What you do is not who you are! The major you choose is not who you are.** You are a tremendously gifted and powerful soul who was dropped on this earth to change it for the better. Live like it, walk like it, and talk like it!

Notes:

_____

_____

_____

_____

_____

_____

_____

_____

Rule #2

Sit in the front of class, and participate actively!

Where you sit in an empty room is a subconscious representation of the way you view yourself in society. For example, if you come into an empty or partially empty classroom and naturally gravitate towards the back of the room to be away from the professor, the action, and the discussion, then that really means that you view yourself in the same manner. In other words, you see yourself on the back end of society, the back end of the action, and on the back end of success. NOT YOU!

You are a powerful student whose voice, opinions, answers, concerns, issues, and comments need to be heard, challenged, celebrated, and recognized. Because of these and many other reasons, this rule is in place. *Well Del, what if all the front seats are taken? Does that mean that I will not get as much out of the class?* Nope, not at all. However, I strongly recommend that you work hard to **be as visible as possible.** Look, you are in college to dominate, to rule, and to take charge of your life and destiny. You don't have time to hang in the back where the instructor's volume and attention tends to fade. You need to be as close to the action as possible.

Let me address the issue of visibility so you can understand what I am talking about. I am not recommending that you try to suck up and come across fake and overly anxious. However, I want you to clearly understand that professors, instructors, and teachers want you to be as hungry for their material as they are to teach it to you. Because of this, you sitting in the front and being involved in classroom discussions and activities **delivers several key messages.**

Classroom & Academic Success

1. **It sends a message to your instructor** that you are positioning yourself for success. It demonstrates that you are concerned about your leadership role in that class.

2. **It sends a message to your classmates** that you are a serious student with a powerful goal of not only getting an A+, but also getting a solid understanding of the material presented.

3. **It sends a message to yourself** to stay engaged in the class and to ensure that your behavior is representative of a leader.

Notes: _____

_____

_____

_____

_____

_____

_____

_____

_____

Delatorro L. McNeal II

Rule #3

Become the first YOU!

One of the biggest reasons why you should be in college and moving systematically through college is to become the first YOU. **Don't waste another day trying to be "the next anybody or anything"... not the next Oprah, Tiger, Bill Gates, Mel Gibson, Beyonce, or anyone else. Become the first, the one, and the only YOU!** There is no one on this earth identical to you. Studies show that even identical twins have many aspects of their personalities that are drastically different.

Make a choice to be the first, the best, the one, and the only you! So many times I talk with college students and ask them why they chose their major. Or, I will ask them why they are members of certain clubs and organizations. The #1 answer to my questions is that someone else said they would be good at it. Another reason is that they are attempting to become someone who is already famous, successful, or renowned.

Now, please understand my point. There is nothing wrong with admiring someone and wanting to possess and exemplify some of their characteristics. In fact, that is very smart. **It is called being *coachable*, which is a critical success trait.** However, there is something wrong with trying to live someone else's dream through your life. There is something wrong with ignoring or downplaying your gifts and talents in hopes of somehow gaining the gifts and talents of someone you admire. You are too special for that.

Always remember, my friend, **you are a world-changer in the making.** You are a trailblazer for the generation that

Delatorro L. McNeal II   7.

comes behind you. **Use every class, every organization, every job, and every opportunity you can to help transform you into the YOU that you have always wanted to be.** Do it for yourself! Not to please parents, kinfolk, or friends. Ultimately, you will be responsible for living out what you create in college. So, create the life that you want and deserve, and your life will reward you greatly in the future.

Notes:

_____

_____

_____

_____

_____

_____

_____

_____

Delatorro L. McNeal II

Rule #4

Form 3-tiered study teams!

You will love this one! I like to use the phrase **"study team"** because it implies a much greater level of productivity and focus than the term "study group". **One of the most powerful secrets to academic success that I used in college and continue to use in business today is the concept of reciprocal learning or what I like to call "iron sharpens iron".** What this means is that when you are forming your study teams, it is critical that you select the right types of persons to help you and your study team become massively successful. Trust me, just because you study with other people does not ensure that you will do well on the test, exam, or project. **I know plenty of people who fail together!** You don't want to fall into this category. So, I want to give you my secret formula for creating and maximizing the 3-Tier Study Team. Recruit and optimize these three types of individuals in your team and you will experience massive success both inside the classroom and out.

First, recruit someone who is MUCH SMARTER than you. I mean, find the student that most of your regular friends think is the "nerd" of the class. You want this person on your team because they will help to further teach, coach, and explain things to you that you did not get from your instructor.

Second, recruit someone who is AS SMART as you. This will probably be one of your friends. You need someone to bounce your ideas off of - someone who thinks similar to you so that you can feel a sense of unity in your understanding of the material that is presented. This person

Delatorro L. McNeal II

9.

also keeps you motivated by showing you that their success could easily be yours too. They rob you of the opportunity to create excuses for your poor performance.

Third, recruit someone who is NOT SMARTER than you. This is, perhaps, the most powerful member of your team. *Why? Won't someone less intelligent slow me down?* NOPE! In fact this person is your greatest blessing. **The true test of whether you know a concept is if you can teach it to someone else.** This person on your team will really test your comprehension and mastery of concepts by making you explain it to them, which will help their understanding - just like your SMARTER friend helps you!

Proactively recruit these 3 people onto your study teams for each subject, maintain them throughout the semester, and you will see just how successful you will become!

Notes: _____

_____

_____

_____

_____

_____

Delatorro L. McNeal II

Rule #5

Challenge your instructors to mentor you!

Paradigm Shift! Professors are not out to FLUNK you! They are not out to get you and make you fail. They may appear firm at times, or even most of the time, but I believe that any instructor worth their salary really wants you to succeed in their class and get out of the material everything that they put into its preparation.

Now, with this understanding, it is important for you to look at your professors as far more than just people that stand and talk to you a few times per week and give assignments and tests. They too, have more meaning to their existence - just as you are far more than a student and far more than a number. **Your professors are far more than lecturers. They have feelings, emotions, ups, downs, families, hard times, personal issues, and successes. They are humans too.** They are more than just assignment-givers, and their ultimate goal in life is NOT to make your college experience "a living hell" as I hear some college students say.

To this end, it is very important that from DAY 1 you make your agenda clear. You need to develop relationships with certain professors that transcend the classroom. You need them to know the WHY in your life. They should know how their class fits into YOUR BIG PICTURE. They need to know how their material, their assignments, projects, and activities are impacting your learning experience.

Quick Secret! Those things on the syllabus are not "Office Hours" – they are **"Mentorship Hours"**! Use them to

Classroom & Academic Success

Delatorro L. McNeal II

11.

build relationship, understanding, and a partnership with your instructors so that you trust them and they trust you. Now, please understand, I am not talking about sucking up to or dating your professor. That is NOT what this book is endorsing AT ALL. **What I am simply saying is to get your instructors personally involved in your success so that they will be advocates for you and a source of support.**

Now, not all professors will welcome your humble attempt. If they don't, try a little harder, but don't go crazy. If there is no hope, squash it and move on. But, be encouraged because **most will welcome your genuine attempt to build relationship** and they will reward your attempt with **attention, encouragement, and hidden success tips** that students who don't use their hours simply DON'T GET!

Notes: _____

_____

_____

_____

_____

_____

_____

Rule #6

Develop an Advisory Board of people who believe in you!

There are people on your college campus, RIGHT NOW, who are meant to be a MAJOR blessing to your college experience. They will believe in your dreams, they will listen to you, they will correct you when you're wrong, and they will help you avoid making a lot of really BIG mistakes. **FIND THESE PEOPLE AND HOLD ON TO THEM.** I can't tell you how important this is. Please, understand that the people I am talking about are not all the vice presidents and presidents of your college or major departments. Many of them come in the form of janitors that clean dorm rooms. It may even be the cashier at the bookstore. Or, it could be the professor that just thinks you're great, even though you have never taken a course from them. **DON'T LET TITLES STAND IN THE WAY OF RELATIONSHIP.**

When you go off to college (whether you stay local or move far away) you still are tasked with the mission of building new relationships and creating an extended family and a new network of success soldiers in your life. **You need a mom away from home. Dr. Brenda Spencer** was one of those persons for me at Florida State University. She encouraged me, opened doors for me, wrote letters of recommendation for me, talked positively about me with other professors BEFORE I took their classes (another great idea), and so much more. Most of all, she simply believed in me and would not allow me to settle for a mediocre college experience.

Dr. Lee Jones was another person who took me under his wing as a son/little brother, and coached me to GREATNESS. He was probably my biggest influence at

Classroom & Academic Success

Florida State and now my career is, in large part, a result of his wisdom, guidance, leadership, support, and mentorship.

My friend, there are people right now...on your campus, waiting for you to find them and latch onto them. These people will help to direct your career, your course selection, your dating relationships, your spiritual journey - you name it! Create an Advisory Board of **POSITIVE PEOPLE WHO SEE MORE** in you **THAN YOU SEE** in yourself. These people will be your greatest asset in college. I promise you. Email them, call them and see how they are doing, take them to lunch, pick their brain, serve them in their departments, and try to get work-study under their supervision. Do what you can to stay connected to them. It will be one of the most powerful tools for success you will have, both in college and beyond.

Notes:

_____

_____

_____

_____

_____

_____

Rule #7

Come Back - Don't burn your bridges!

You would be absolutely amazed at the number of students who come to class with a great instructor, learn a lot, grow a lot, and experience a lot. But once the course is over, that's it. **The instructor or professor NEVER hears from the student again. I mean NEVER. What an insult – but what a reality.** What I have learned is that the thing that separates the good students from the great students is that **the great students COME BACK.** They stop back by every now and then just to give updates and ask for additional insight.

In the Fall of 2002, I became an Adjunct Professor of Public Speaking in the Department of Communication at The University of South Florida. I loved it! My first class consisted of a group of about 35 students in a state-of-the-art training facility on campus. It was great! **As a result of the skills they learned, every student developed a great deal and became powerful voices on campus. However, after the program was over, only 1 STUDENT kept in regular contact with me.** To be honest, it was the student that I LEAST expected to keep in touch with anyone – let alone myself. He was a loner. However, at least once every 2 months he would stop by my office to just talk, get updates, and share his successes. I was glad to see him, but I would always ask myself, "Why don't the other students stop by?"

What I learned is that most people are only cognizant of relationships that they can see. **However, truly great people have a way of keeping in touch with the people that change their lives regardless of time.** Do yourself a

Classroom & Academic Success

favor, my friend. STAY IN TOUCH with the instructors that really make a major impact on your life. You simply NEVER KNOW when you will need them to support you further in your college or professional career. Don't let your instructors "have it" once the course is over. Tell them now how you feel, but keep it constructive. You never know how that seed can come back to grow into a piece of fruit that feeds you later. Quick example, I had a professor that I thought was super tough, at first. But, after I got an A in his course, he believed in my goals and dreams so much that he kept me in mind. Months later, he told his son, the CEO of a local company, about me and **I was hired "on the spot" as an Intern the following semester!** You just never know. So, remember to stay in touch and don't burn your bridges.

Notes:

_____

_____

_____

_____

_____

_____

_____

Chapter 2
Club & Organization Success

Rule #1

Go where you're celebrated, not where you're tolerated!

Listen, I know you want to fit in. I know you want to make a difference. I also know you want your voice to be heard and used to create positive change. However, please understand that on a college campus there are potentially 10, 50, or up to 300 different organizations & clubs that you can become involved in - some good and some bad. **Some will develop you and some will bankrupt you. Some will help you to create a future, while others will destroy your future.** So, it is important that you ask yourself several key questions before you join a club or organization. In addition, you must understand who you are and what you represent. If not, joining an organization can define that **for you** – which can be **very dangerous.**

I can vividly remember wanting to join a specific organization so badly. I was focused on that more than anything else. I even let it take the place of my spiritual growth. Well, God had other plans because that same organization I wanted to join ultimately turned on me for no reason. I like to refer to it as being "black-balled". **I was devastated!** I tried to do everything I could to fit in. However, one of my mentors in college helped me understand one day that **"We must go where we are celebrated, not where we are tolerated".** I had to learn how to discover that special place where my gifts and talents would be welcomed and encouraged. It was my job to find that place and maximize my experience once I got there. The next semester **I went where I was celebrated,** and became president of the organization within 1 year. That was a major promotion for me, because I had found a place where my natural gifts flourished. I was the first ever president of the FSU Gospel

Clubs & Organizations

Choir to be re-elected 3 consecutive years!

So, ask yourself and your advisory board these 4 important questions before you join any major club or organization on campus.

1. Is there a clear connection between the purpose of this organization and my purpose that would facilitate membership?

2. What do I expect to contribute and gain from this membership that will get me closer to my college and career goals?

3. What characteristics in the leadership of the organization have I seen that I like and would like to aspire towards?

4. What will membership cost me in terms of time, talents, money, and reputation, and is the return on investment a positive one?

Notes:

_____

_____

_____

_____

_____

Delatorro L. McNeal II

Rule #2

Join to create lasting positive change!

Now, before you join, I have a major question to ask you.

WHY?

It is very critical for you to have a powerful answer to this question. Just as you must have a strong WHY for your major selection and a strong WHY for even attending college in the first place, you must also have a strong WHY for joining a club or organization. **Members without a strong WHY are DEADWEIGHT to the leadership of any club or organization.** Every position serves a purpose and every member should be in attendance on purpose. Make sure that your motives for joining are pure. If not, you won't last long and the REAL you will shine through eventually. You see, in the last rule I was trying to join an organization for many of the **WRONG reasons.** I wanted popularity, notoriety, fame, respect, women, status, power, belonging, a title, recognition, and credibility as a freshman.

Well, these carnal motives, I believe, are the things that kept me from being accepted into that organization. **In hindsight, however, I am so GLAD that I got rejected. I later learned that I did not need that organization to make me.** I also realized that when I became a part of the organization where I was celebrated, I had an overwhelming desire to serve, give back, make a difference, help people pursue their dreams, build a strong team, and all that great stuff. **Since my motives were pure and positive, my acceleration and impact within the organization was rapid and long lasting.**

Clubs & Organizations

What is your mission for joining the organization? **An organization is just like an elevator. It will either take you up or it will take you down.** Before you get on an elevator, you already know in which direction you need to go and what floor you need to get off on. Well, know which direction you want to go before joining a club/organization and know, from the beginning, the end result you would like to see come from your empowered involvement.

Notes:

_____

_____

_____

_____

_____

_____

_____

_____

Rule #3

Build an organization on purpose and principle, not personality!

We will be talking in great detail about leadership later in this book, but I would like to mention a key component of leadership here. **Since you are a destined, determined, and highly motivated student, it very likely that you will be called to lead different aspects of the organization.** You will probably be chosen to head up certain events, projects, programs, or committees. It is very important for you to build your organization. You may not be the president, but it is still vital that you help to build the organization and every assignment within it, **while using purpose and principle as your guides - not personality.**

Have you ever been a part of a group where the leader was strong and well liked, but when the leader left, the group split? I am sure that you have. *Have you ever seen an organization that was doing well, but the leadership graduated or changed organizations and because of that, the organization took a major downturn?* Well, I have seen that happen many times and still see it on college campuses today. Why does this happen? **The answer is that individuals are building organizations based on people and personality, rather than on purpose and principle.**

The purpose and principle of an organization should be the foundation upon which all activities, events, and programs are built. **The true test of good leadership is NOT the condition of the organization when the leader is present. The true test of good leadership is the condition of the organization in the ABSENCE of the leader.** In other words, if your organization fails once

Clubs & Organizations

you leave, don't be impressed with yourself and say things like "I knew that they couldn't make it without me". **The reality is, my friend, if it failed when you left, YOU WERE THE REAL FAILURE.**

Always remember, you are building a living, breathing organization that has its own purpose and destiny. **Your gifts and talents should be used to strengthen the organization permanently.** Policies you implement, procedures you create, and precedents you set should ultimately benefit the organization first and your popularity and ego last.

Notes:

_____

_____

_____

_____

_____

_____

_____

_____

Rule #4

Graduate with a degree, not a title or a position!

With the plethora of exciting and challenging organizations that there are to get involved in at college, sometimes it can be tempting to shift your academic priorities for the purposes of bettering the organization. Now, there is nothing wrong with earmarking time in your schedule for organizational activities, meetings, events, and celebrations. These gatherings are all important and have their place in your college experience. However, allow me to remind you of something very important. **You are in college to graduate with a degree and purpose-driven career path, NOT a title or position.**

So often, I hear how students "accidentally" extend their college careers by 1, 2, and even 3 semesters - NOT because of academic or financial challenges, but because they put clubs and organizations before their education and courses of study. **Priorities in your life should be based on purpose!** Therefore, always remember the overall purpose for your college experience and keep your perspective regardless of how *"change the world"* that club or organization sounds.

Now, truth be told, getting a 4.0 GPA should NOT be your only aim either. Companies today are looking for people who are "well-rounded" in their collegiate experience. This means that they want someone who not only can study, but also someone who can work well with teams, understand and negotiate the pressures of implementing major projects, balance multiple commitments, interface with diverse cultures respectively, and so forth. Being a powerful and productive member of **THE RIGHT clubs and organizations** can help you to develop these and many other major success skills.

Clubs & Organizations

Now, it is also critical for you to understand that you don't want to go to college only to attempt to build a resume that will attract companies. NO...NO...NO! You want to build a resume and a portfolio of skills that YOU are impressed, inspired, and motivated by. Remember, you must *Write Your Own Ticket* to be ultimately successful. One day you may **HIRE YOURSELF!**

So just remember to keep all your extracurricular activities in proper balance and you will be very successful both in college and beyond.

Notes: _____

_____

_____

_____

_____

_____

_____

_____

Rule #5

Pick organizations that supplement your learning!

There are a large number of clubs and organizations that will not only allow you to build your resume and your portfolio of skills, but also provide some major opportunities for you to showcase your gifts and talents. There are many organizations with local chapters that have national and international prominence. Becoming a member of these types of organizations does several key things for you.

1. It provides you with an **immediate professional outlet** for you to attach yourself to and begin to build credibility.

2. It creates **opportunities for you to travel and experience** the width and breadth of what national exposure provides.

3. It gives you a real-life organization upon which to **immediately apply many of the theoretical principles** that you are learning in the classroom.

4. When affiliated with the right types of organizations – it stops you from asking the disempowering questions of *"Why am I learning this?"* and *"When will I ever use this information?"*

When I was in junior high and high school, I played football. I can remember those long and challenging practices like they happened yesterday. But, the one thing that I remember most is that whenever the coach wanted to teach us a new play or skill for the coming game, he would teach us the play, strategy, or technique first. Then, for another 2 hours, we would put that skill into PRACTICE. **Repetition is the mother of skill. Rehearsal is the father of learning.** Never forget that.

Clubs & Organizations

Delatorro L. McNeal II

27.

Being actively involved in the right clubs and organizations allows you to immediately put into **PRACTICE all that you are learning inside the classroom. It's one thing to read a book on leadership; it's another thing to successfully lead a group of your peers to accomplish a common goal.** The right organizations can very powerfully take you **from thinking to trying, from dreaming to doing, from wanting to walking, and from pontification to participation.** Go out there and show the world what you have to offer. **Just remember, clubs and organizations are ALWAYS the side dishes and NEVER the main course. In the wise words of Mr. Miyagi, "Stay FOCUSED Danielson!"**

Notes:

_____

_____

_____

_____

_____

_____

_____

Delatorro L. McNeal II

Chapter 3
Financial & Credit Success

Rule #1

Pursue the all mighty DESTINY, not the all mighty dollar!

My friend, this is probably the most important rule of the entire book. While in college, DON'T LET MONEY BE YOUR ONLY FOCUS FOR SUCCESS! **Although important, IF MONEY IS THE ONLY MAJOR MOTIVATOR FOR YOUR COLLEGE EXPERIENCE, YOU WILL NOT MASTER THE "WRITE YOUR OWN TICKET" TECHNIQUES.**

Listen, there are roughly 12 million students across the U.S. pursuing college degrees yearly. When you ask most students why they have chosen their major, their response is that their major will lead them to making good money. Money is great, money is important, and money is a major necessity of life. But, **MONEY IS ONLY A TEMPORARY MOTIVATOR.** For most people, as soon as they earn more, they spend more. It's a concept called **"Expenses Rise to Meet Income".** What this simply means is that as soon as most people start making more money, naturally, their wants and desires fluctuate or swell up to accommodate the income bracket they now exist within. The problem arises when people spend a large portion of their lives pursuing money rather than purpose and destiny. They ultimately end up working dead-end jobs while earning barely enough money to pay the bills. They spend their entire lives "working to pay bills", and that is no way to live.

MILLIONS of Americans are sucked into this viscous trap, because they put the pursuit of money before the pursuit of their passion. You can make money doing anything. If you get good enough at it, and get the right person to see you doing the right thing at the right time, you can make money doing anything. But, it's not all about the money. It is about the fact that you have a powerful purpose in life. **Money can make you feel "successful" but it won't make you feel "significant" until you understand the purpose for that money in your life.** Be in college pursuing the **ACADEMIC CREDIENTIALS** of your **Natural Gifting!**

Do what you love to do - what you were born to do - and I will teach you how to find someone who will pay you to do it!

Notes:

_____

_____

_____

_____

_____

_____

_____

_____

Delatorro L. McNeal II

Rule #2

Create and sustain multiple income streams!

Listen my friend, what I am about to teach you and tell you will CHANGE YOUR LIFE FOREVER IF YOU CAN UNDERSTAND IT AND RUN WITH IT! Are you ready?

Here it is!!! **You were never meant to live off of just one income stream.** The days of dad bringing home the bacon and mom frying it up in a pan (or vice versa) are OVER! Most families in America need dual incomes just to survive. In today's market, raises are too minimal and prices are too fluctuating to even attempt to keep up. This is not a negative thing. However, it is a reality. I go into major corporations and speak all the time. The #1 complaint I get from employees is the fact that they don't make enough money. EVERYONE WANTS MORE MONEY. So, you as an empowered young adult need to begin to think from the standpoint of abundant income streams rather than a scarcity of them.

Many people in life operate on the scarcity mentality. Jobs are scarce, good relationships are scarce, promotions are scarce, job security is scarce, and the list goes on and on. So, why frustrate yourself by trying to get in the same scarce line for your 3% raise like everyone else? No...No...No. There is a much more effective way! **Begin to think ABUNDANCE. Money is abundant, opportunity is abundant, quality relationships are abundant (if you know where to look), love is abundant, joy is abundant, your dream is abundant, information is abundant – and so are you.**

Now, in order to live the abundant life you need to learn how to add an additional income stream or streams to your life. **Listen, my friend. If money can go OUT of your bank account in multiple ways, why can't it come IN via multiple ways?** In other words, begin to think how you can use your "outside of class and study time" to bring in funds from other sources.

For example, part-time jobs, investments, side-jobs, weekend work, babysitting, property, Internet businesses, multi-level marketing jobs, errand running, and the like. There are so many ways to add more income into your life. While in college and even afterwards, think of additional ways to bring funds into your household, and you will feel so much more freedom financially, personally, professionally, spiritually, and socially.

Notes: _____

_____

_____

_____

_____

_____

_____

Rule #3

Find people to pay you to be a student!

Listen, I say *"If you are gonna be a student, you might as well find people who will pay you to be one!"* Now, when I say "pay you to be a student", what I mean is that the job will require you to do what you would already be doing as a regular student – with a few extra tasks. Think about scholarships, assistantships, work-study, and directed individual studies. All of these methods help you get paid to study, research, manage, supervise, assist, administrate, and the like.

There are a wide variety of jobs and organizations that will pay you to be a student. For example, I was a Resident Assistant (RA) for 1.5 years of my college career. Now, as an RA I did not get a bi-weekly paycheck. **However, I did get room and board FREE.** I never had to pay for food or rent for 1.5 years. That is a huge savings in college! Also, I got a lot of other perks that saved me money, such as special privileges with technology, special parking, discounts within my college town, and other really good stuff. Not to mention, I was getting great experience learning property management, people skills, negotiation skills, money management skills, interviewing skills, and a host of other qualities.

Another example came in graduate school; I had a job as a Resource Center Supervisor. It was my job to open the center for students, check out books, check IDs of students who wanted to use the computer lab, and maintain other student employee schedules. It was super easy and I loved it. I did 4 hour days – 5 days per week. **That is 20 hours per week. But of those 20 hours, I studied, wrote papers, and did my own research for about 15 of those hours each week. IT WAS AWESOME!** When I was not helping students, I would

Financial & Credit Success

simply do the work that I would normally do at home. In terms of perks, when the center was closed off to students, I still had access. I was paid to be the student I already was. You can have the same type of success that I did. You just need to look for the opportunities and ask your mentors to help you find them as well. Search bulletin boards, newspapers, and job posting locations for **opportunities to do what you do best – be a student.** If you can do that, then I will help you find someone to pay you to do it!

Notes:

_____

_____

_____

_____

_____

_____

_____

_____

Rule #4

Invest in financial wisdom!

While we are talking about finances, this rule is a very important one. You must learn how to think differently about money. **First of all, instead of using the word "spend" replace it in your vocabulary with the word "INVEST".** This is very important. When you spend money, you don't necessarily know where it goes, nor do you really care. You just spend your money like you do your time, and for many people that equals waste. However, when you invest in something, you have a totally different expectation. **You want something in return for what you invest** and you are expecting your return to be in greater measure than what you invested. For example, if you spend $20 on a pizza, in exchange for your $20 you got a hot, fresh, delicious pizza that hopefully satisfied your hunger. It was an equal trade. However, hours later you will be hungry again. On the other hand, if you invest $20 in a bank account, your expectation is that several years from now you will get back more than what you put in.

Well, the same is true about wisdom. My friend, please understand something. **You must learn how to invest in wisdom** - not just knowledge. *Well Del, aren't wisdom and knowledge the same?* No my friend, **because Wisdom includes knowledge AND the WISE use of it!**

Begin to think of ways that you can use the information you get, for your benefit. **Do me a favor. ALWAYS invest more into what goes IN you than you do into what goes ON you.** What I mean is, if you are willing to spend $50 on pair of new fashionable shoes (what goes on you), but you are not willing to invest $50 to attend a seminar or

Financial & Credit Success

conference or to purchase motivational material (what goes in you), then something is very wrong. It is not the things that go on you that make you valuable. **It is the content of what is on the inside of you (i.e., character, determination, focus, willpower, attitude, integrity, etc.) that makes you priceless.** Any chance you get, you should be buying books, tapes, seminars, and other learning opportunities to further your understanding of finances, how this world works, and how money can be a very powerful tool to get the things you need. One of the greatest lessons I learned about money is this: **Money only makes you more of what you already are! Money Magnifies.** That is either good or it's bad depending on the person. Invest in yourself, my friend. Invest in your greatness and others will see it and celebrate it. **Money with a positive purpose behind it = POWER!**

Notes: _____

_____

_____

_____

_____

_____

_____

Delatorro L. McNeal II

Rule #5

Think ROI - Be smarter than I was!

As a piggyback to the last rule, this rule is very important. **ROI stands for Return On Investment.** If you want to be successful in life, in college, and beyond, you must understand that you should EXPECT a solid return or a benefit from the things you invest in. Think about it for a quick second. One of the major reasons why most people even attend college in the first place is because we have been socialized to believe that the return on investment from a college education and degree is a secure job with a secure income for the rest of our lives. **Well, any blind person can see that our economy and the workforce have changed so much until those luxuries of life are no longer as secure as they used to be.** That is why I stress the importance of the WHY in your life. The return on investment for your studying, reading, writing, stressing about tests, cramming, penny-pinching, and all that **should be a lot more than just a fancy piece of paper with computerized signatures and the school seal on it.**

Now please understand, I am not degrading the value of a college education. Remember, I got one – two actually. What I am saying is that my college education was about so much more than the degree - **and so it should be for you. Millions of successful people around the world can prove to you that you don't NEED college to be successful.** There are also millions of other successful people who will prove to you that you do. The point is this. You need to expect more from yourself and from your college experience investment than just a piece of paper and a resume filler. In the same vain, you should expect more from your finances than just some immediate return. For example, my

Financial & Credit Success

junior year in college, I traded in my Nissan Stanza for a new Honda Civic LX. The only problem was that I leased the Civic. **In fact, after my 2-year lease was up, I leased it again- that time for 3 years. Which means that I leased (rented) a car for 5 years and still owed on it when the lease was up. THAT WAS SO STUPID!** In addition, a few weeks after I leased it the first time, I used a part of my scholarship money to buy rims to go on my rented car.

So, I owned rims but I leased and re-leased the car. Why? I did it because I wanted the return on my investment to be people thinking I was cool and ladies thinking I had a nice ride. The smart thing would have been to put $1,000 down on the purchase of the Honda, rather than leasing it. I was so stupid, but I did it because I could. Listen, my friend. Just because you can do something financially does not always mean you should! Use wisdom and always **THINK RETURN ON INVESTMENT.**

Notes:

_____

_____

_____

_____

_____

Be a giver, because givers get!

My friend, it is so important that you learn one powerful secret about money and finance. **GIVERS GET! People who have a lifestyle of giving also have a lifestyle of receiving.** They just do. It's like the boomerang effect. When you throw a boomerang with any force, in any direction, it will come back to you in the same way that it went away from you. Well, the same is true for money. **When you give money to stupid and pointless things, it returns to you in stupid and pointless ways. However, when you give money towards good, worthy, and important things, it comes back to you in good, worthy, and important ways.**

A closed fist does not get anything - but an open hand does! You must put yourself in the posture to give, in order to be proactively in the posture to receive. I am going to teach you a few things that my millionaire mentors taught me about being a giver. Do you know that many self-made millionaires in this country are givers? In fact, they have a special term that they use. It is a spiritual term **called tithing**. People who are **tithers** give 10% of their earnings away to a charitable or non-profit cause. Whatever they make, they automatically donate a percentage of 10% or greater to that organization. Why? Well, because most successful people understand that givers get! For example, so many people talk negatively about Bill Gates and how wealthy he is. He is worth multiple-billions of dollars. However, do you know that he donates or gives away over $800 million dollars per year? Givers get! *Okay Del, all that is great, but how does that apply to me as a college student?* Great Question. I want to challenge you to do what millionaires and aspiring millionaires do. Become a giver through the sowing of your time, talents and treasures. Find a worthy cause, church, spiritual organization, or non-profit to donate 10% of your income and time towards, and watch how you will begin to receive in a greater measure than what you gave. When I was in college I tithed on my paychecks and my financial aid surplus checks. I am not recommending tithing on loans because that is not your money. But, I do suggest that you find an outlet for a portion of your treasure, talents, and time and watch it come back to your life in ways that you would have never thought possible. **I give 10% of my time, talents, and treasures to great causes in my community and it all comes back to BLESS me INDEED!** You can do the same as well.

Notes:

_____

_____

_____

_____

_____

_____

_____

Delatorro L. McNeal II

Realize that the FREE T-Shirt is NOT Worth It!

AVOID the CREDIT CARD TRAP!
AVOID the CREDIT CARD TRAP!
AVOID the CREDIT CARD TRAP!
AVOID the CREDIT CARD TRAP!

My friend, listen to me. I don't care what those people in the student union on your campus offer you; DON'T open multiple credit card accounts just to get free t-shirts, teddy bears, or dinner for 2 at a nice restaurant. **The financial decisions you make in college could have lasting negative impacts on your credit score or lasting positive impacts on your credit score.** I totally underestimated how important my credit score was in college. Now, truth be told, I was doing very well managing my credit debt in college. I had a great credit score in the 700s, but it was shortly after college when I got a little careless with my credit card spending. Things are all good now, but I did have some pitfalls along the way.

Implement this rule when it comes to credit card spending and you will be successful both in college and beyond. **First, don't put things on credit that are wants; only put things on credit that are needs.** Rims are wants. Super nice clothes are wants. Super fancy vacations are wants. Books, seminars, educational trainings are needs. Shelter is a need. Underwear and clean clothes are needs. **Learn the difference between a want and a need,** and you will not end up in the credit card trap. Also, if you have trouble disciplining yourself not to spend money on credit when you go to the mall, **then leave your credit cards at home.** Another trick is to put your credit cards at the bottom of a jar of water. Then put that jar in the freezer. When you really want to buy something on credit, pull the jar out. It will probably take almost 24-hours for all the ice to liquefy so you can reach down to get the card. If after you have thought clearly about the importance of that item and you still NEED to use someone else's money to buy it, then go for it. Another great tip is to ask your mentors and advisory team about a major purchase before you invest

Financial & Credit Success

in it.

Also, make sure that you pay your bills ON TIME. Making a habit of not doing so, will lower your credit score and collections will remain on your credit report for 7 years. I know plenty of people who are still suffering from lower than usual credit scores. Not from things they did last year, but from things they did **5 years ago. CREDIT IS NO JOKE.** Protect your credit, protect your wallet/purse, and protect your identity.

Be careful who you share your social security number with. **NEVER GIVE AWAY YOUR SOCIAL SECURITY NUMBER JUST SO THAT A "FRIEND" OF YOURS CAN REGISTER YOU FOR A CLASS.** You would not imagine how many students credit reports get absolutely "jacked up" because of that one simple mistake. Don't trust people with your personal government-issued information.

Carry one credit card with a low limit of $500 on it. **Only charge items that you can pay off within 30 days.** If it is an absolute emergency and your parents or loved ones will not help you pay for it, then at least charge it on a low interest credit card. Oh, while I am talking about interest, please keep this in mind. **Interest is calculated on your debt DAILY.** So when you get the money, don't wait for the statement, pay that bad boy off as soon as you can. **Remember, credit card money is NOT YOUR MONEY. It belongs to someone else.** Additionally, if you go to the mall and buy $300 worth of clothes and you save **10% by opening up a Store Credit Card, that has an interest rate of 19% - YOU ARE NOT SAVING ANYTHING.** They just got over on you. They are now making an additional 9% on top of what they profited off of you buying the clothes to begin with. **USE WISDOM MY FRIEND.** Don't fall for those tricks that stores try to use to get you to open up unneeded charge card accounts. They are all gimmicks to get you to keep spending money with them.

Delatorro L. McNeal II

Another great tip about money and credit. **Apartments not maintained properly can JACK UP YOUR CREDIT.** Make sure that if you have a roommate, you have **SEPARATE LEASES on that apartment.** Also, ensure that each lease is separated by separate social security numbers. You don't want to have negative information on your credit that was your roommate's doing. **Additionally, KNOW HOW TO LIVE WITHIN YOUR MEANS. Your rent payment should only be 28% of your monthly income.** So if you earn $1,000 per month, you should only be paying $280 of that in rent. If you make $2,000 per month, you should be paying about $560 per month in rent. Oh, and don't use STUDENT LOANS to buy new cars, stay in fancy apartments, or purchase fancy clothes. REMEMBER THAT IS NOT YOUR MONEY. It belongs to someone else. You want to live a very comfortable life after college. **So be WISE and INVEST YOUR MONEY SMART.** Why? Because the free shirt, simply is not worth it!

Notes:

Financial & Credit Success

Chapter 4
Relationship Success

Rule #1

Evaluate the people in your life regularly

Never forget that during the entire time you live on this earth, you are in the people management business. There are people constantly coming in and out of your life. Everyday you are meeting, mingling with, waving to, standing beside, talking to, interacting with, studying with, working with, and assessing people. You are a direct result of the types of people that you hang with. **In fact, studies have shown that people tend to earn within $5,000 of their close friends.** This means that in order for you to *"Write your own ticket for wealth"* and live a life that being financially strapped is not a part of, it is critical that you begin to surround yourself with people who are movers and shakers. You need people in your life who have your best interest at heart and who are willing to put their action where their mouth is. In college, you are going to meet 3 types of bones. You will meet **"Wishbones"**. These are people who dream about success, wish for success, and imagine success - and that's it. There's no follow through, no focus, and no commitment. You will also meet **"Jawbones"**. These are people who will just talk about it, gossip about it, and brag about it, but still never really implement what they say. These people blow a lot of smoke, but there is some great news. You will also meet a third type of bones, whom I like to call **"Backbones"**. These are people who have enough grit, determination, focus, and power to **ACT on what they say and CREATE the life that they want.**

People are just like elevators; they can either take you up or down. So, keep your circle of friends positive. Keep your study teams positive. Keep the people you date positive. Keep the people you work with positive.

Relationship Success

Oh, and don't pay people to bring you down! *What does that mean Del?* Great question! Don't pay large cell phone or long distance telephone bills talking to people who are negative, self-defeating, discouraging, and who literally drain your enthusiasm each time you deal with them. **Take the cell phone test.** Each semester, make a list of the people that are stored in your cell phone. For the positive people, rate them a plus (+). For the negative people, rate them a minus (-). Then work to remove yourself from the negative people in your life, in order to maximize the power of your positive associations.

Think clearly and deliberately before giving people your cell phone number. Because once someone has your cell phone number, they literally have 24/7 access to you. Now, why give negative people 24/7 access to bring you down even further? Pointless right? RIGHT! So do what you must to protect your positivity.

Notes: _____

_____

_____

_____

_____

_____

Rule #2

Create lasting friendships based on honesty & integrity!

College provides a wonderful opportunity for you to meet, interact, and develop strong relationships with people from literally all over the world. People will come into your life for a reason, a season, and also for a lifetime. You need to know the reason why people enter and exit your life. *Are they supposed to teach you something? Are you supposed to teach them something? Are they supposed to help you get through an obstacle you will encounter somewhere in the future?* People will also come into your life for a season. That season could last one class period, one semester, one year, or one decade. You may never know the length of the season, but you MUST know this. **You have the power to pull people into and drive people out of your circle of influence.** Be smart and use wisdom. Don't develop relationships with people based on their popularity, style of dress, money, or any of these flaky, external, and conditional reasons. Team up with friends who are positive - both young and old – and focus on their internal characteristics, which are built upon solid personality traits.

I can save you years of heartache by encouraging you to make quality decisions about your friendships that are not always the easiest to see externally, but that do exist internally. Think about qualities such as character, integrity, consistency, honesty, determination, loyalty, ambition, focus, commitment, virtue, honor, and self-worth. You see, these traits don't hang off of our bodies like arms, legs, butts, breasts, and everything else that we use to qualify whether or not someone is attractive. Hello! **In order to see the real stuff, you have to look beyond the externally attractive frame to see the quality and strength of the internal individual.**

Relationship Success

Delatorro L. McNeal II

51.

You have the power to keep positive people in your life. Yes you do! **You have the power to disassociate and minimize your connection with toxic and self-sabotaging individuals who do nothing for your dream but slowly kill it.** You have the power to create connections with people who will benefit your life for many years to come. For example, you will become a part of your college's alumni association when you graduate. For the most part, professional alumni look out for each other. Friendships, like houses, should be built on a solid foundation (e.g., trust, love, integrity, etc.), that will last at the conception, through the duration, and at the culmination of your college experience.

Notes:

_____

_____

_____

_____

_____

_____

_____

Rule #3

Open your eyes and celebrate diversity!

My first roommate slept naked! My first next-door neighbor in college was a white man with a confederate flag hanging in his room and several shotguns. My first study team in college consisted of 2 Caucasian students, 1 Indian student, 1 Korean student, and myself. What am I trying to tell you? Open your eyes and celebrate the vast array of diversity that exists on your campus. **Life would be very boring if everyone looked, talked, walked, studied, and dressed exactly like you. The people around you are there to challenge your conceptualization of "the norm".** Some of the greatest lessons you will learn about life will come from people who don't look or talk anything like you. **Some of your most enriching conversations will be had in the midst of people who CAN'T relate to the way that you were raised.** That is okay; in fact, that is a great thing.

Remember the guy that had the confederate flag, the shotguns, and looked like a skinhead by his own admission? Well, his name was Ben Benedict and **he ended up being one of my very best friends in college.** I was black, young, and focused. He was white, loud, and wild. However, once we looked past what made us different and began to respect each others' worlds, we grew so close that he cried when I moved out of my dorm 2 years later.

Don't forget, being prejudice has little to do with race and everything to do with a premature perception of someone or something else. Don't prejudge people just because they don't dress like you, speak like you, or demonstrate the same habits that you do. The

Relationship Success

reality is that there are a rainbow of people in this world who can impact your life. **So, make good decisions that are based on "content of character" rather than "color of skin" as my man, Dr. Martin Luther King Jr., would say.**

Listen, my friend. College provides a great opportunity for you to learn a great deal about a variety of different cultures, customs, and traditions. DON'T go "buck wild", and get all crazy (we will talk about that in the next rule). DO learn about and celebrate the diversity that exists around you. Learn a new dance, play a different instrument, go to a Gospel concert, take a foreign cuisine class, and other kinds of cool and different stuff. Participate in activities that stretch your paradigms and expand your understanding of this great world that we are blessed to be a part of.

Notes:

_____

_____

_____

_____

_____

_____

Delatorro L. McNeal II

Rule #4

Never compromise your greatness for others!

My friend, please read this rule over multiple times. This rule is very important for the success of your greatness in college and beyond. Your greatness – the destiny, purpose, plan, call, and personality that you have been uniquely gifted with– is so very special that when you were born…**the mold was broken.** That means, you will never find anyone in this world exactly like you. Your greatness – your smile, your laugh, your wit, and your natural gifts and talents – are so customized that others can imitate you, but they can never duplicate you. To this end, please listen to Big Brother Del. **NEVER COMPROMISE YOUR GREATNESS. Don't sell out on your dream and your destiny just to be liked, popular, accepted, initiated, given a scholarship…none of these things.** Don't compromise how awesome you are for anyone or anything.

Don't compromise your body! Your body was created to be enjoyed by the person you marry. To tell you the truth, I got this wrong several times in college. I won't even lie. But I have also had to pay the price for it. I didn't get any diseases or anything like that. Rather, I've endured emotional scares, memories I can't erase, and the regret of not being the brand new showroom automobile that my wife deserved. **By the time I got to her, I was a used vehicle in great condition. However, that did not dismiss the fact that I was used. I hope you can get my analogy.** Don't date anyone who does not treat you like the awesome and blessed young adult that you are. Don't allow any instructor to hold a grade over your head to get you to compromise your greatness. Don't let any popular social clubs make you give in to something that you KNOW is

Relationship Success

wrong and inappropriate. **Listen, you don't have to drink, do drugs, or sleep around to be popular, to be the LIFE of the party, or any of those "cool" things. Just be you,** and find people who will appreciate how awesome you are. At first, the chair of compromise is very comfortable. However, in the long run, it is also the chair that will lead to a crappy life that you settled for. Instead, pick the chair of commitment. It is not nearly as comfortable or popular, but remember this. Those who choose to sit in the chair of compromise now - will ultimately work for those who sacrificed to sit in the chair of commitment. **If you commit to your dream, your dream will commit to you and the world will be touched by the impact you make.**

Notes: _____

_____

_____

_____

_____

_____

_____

Rule #5

Be on a Mission ... Or you will become the mission of someone else!

Decide - right now - that you are a **person on a mission.** Make a deliberate and determined decision that you are not just someone aimlessly walking around campus waiting for a "hook up". **Rather, you are a focused, intelligent, and dedicated individual who is walking through the journey of your college experience to accomplish a special mission.** There are certain things you must do in preparation for your mission. You chart your course, come up with a plan of attack, and recruit talented people who can help you do more than you could do on your own. You also keep quiet about the mission and only tell those who can help you achieve it. You execute the plan and keep all your team members in regular communication so that if your plan changes, everyone can refocus and re-strategize.

You must look at college as your special mission. If you choose to accept your mission, you must turn into a **"special agent"** - an agent of change, success, and progress.

Without a mission you have no purpose. Without a purpose in the game of life, my friend, you are sitting on the sidelines instead of actively participating in your destiny. **Without a mission, it is easy to settle for playing a supporting role in someone else's drama.** You quickly become a pawn on someone else's chess table – used for their selfish motives and ambitions. **YOU ARE TOO GREAT FOR THAT.** Be on a mission when you go to class. Be on a mission when you join an organization. Be on a mission when you study and prepare for projects and assignments. **Be on a mission when you date and search for the person that will help you walk through this journey of life.**

Relationship Success

Delatorro L. McNeal II

57.

Be on a mission to graduate college debt free. Be on a mission to learn and **APPLY every strategy that you can,** so that you will graduate and focus on CHANGING the World one life at a time.

Notes:

_____

_____

_____

_____

_____

_____

_____

_____

Delatorro L. McNeal II

Chapter 5
Major Selection Success

Discover your Purpose & Passion, and then Major in it!

The only person that can live your life is you! Therefore, it is very important for you to understand that outside influences are not always the best benchmarks for determining your success. **Your major in college SHOULD ONLY BE a field of study that confirms and supports the natural gifts and talents you were born with.** Stop thinking MAJOR = MONEY & HAPPINESS because it does not. I know many professionals today who spend hundreds of thousands of dollars earning law degrees (just an example) only to practice for 2 years, hate it, and then go into a totally different field having NOTHING to do with law. MAJOR does not equal MONEY & HAPPINESS.

PURPOSE + PASSION + PROFICINCEY = BIG MONEY & HAPPINESS

In other words, once you discover what you were born to do (purpose), pursue that thing with all your heart (passion), and master your passion so much that you know it backwards and forwards (proficiency). THEN I can promise, my friend, that you will find plenty of people who will pay you to do it. *Well Del, how do I discover my purpose?* **Great question. In my second book, Robbing the Grave of Its Greatness, 8 Steps to Birthing Your Best Right Now** I dedicated an entire chapter towards helping people discover their purpose and passion in life. Visit my website **www.delmcneal.com** and order this book for yourself and that chapter will guide you step-by-step on how to discover and uncover your mission in this thing called life.

Major Selection Success

Let me tell you something else. **Every purpose and passion does not always fit neatly into a specific major at a college. In fact, there are many purposes that don't fit perfectly... MINE DIDN'T.** Florida State does not offer a major in Professional Motivational Speaking. I could not get my BS, MS, or Ph.D in that field. So, I had to pick the closest major, which was Interpersonal & Speech Communication. I took semester-long courses on subjects like Public Speaking, Applied Voice & Diction, Articulation, Listening, Counseling, Drama, and the list goes on and on. In graduate school, I picked Human Performance Enhancement Technology as my M.S. degree focus because I wanted to learn how to enhance the performance of people in my audiences. Are you starting to see the point? So, if your passion and purpose do not fit in a nice and neat degree program, don't fret. Just do the best you can with the programs of study offered by customizing your college experience with courses that match closely to what you ultimately want to do. **Wow, I am so excited for you!**

Notes:

_____

_____

_____

_____

Rule #2

When college gets hard, work it hard!

College degrees are not the easiest things to come by these days. It takes hard work, focus, sacrifice, finances, long-suffering, patience, and a lot of other stuff. **So, when college gets hard - and it will - work it hard!** College will make you get creative with your finances. College will make you decide how you feel about your faith and spiritual beliefs. College will drive you crazy sometimes and make you want to give up. When I say college, I am not just talking about class. I am talking about financial aid, roommates, leadership organizations, parties, social events, family situations, money problems, and all the other bonuses that come along with the college experience. Many times, people QUIT when things get hard. **The 2 hardest things to do in life are to START and to FINISH.** Therefore, I want to challenge you to **Start what you Finish and Finish what you Start.** Start the things that finish in your mind by acting on them. Finish the things you start by persisting and persevering during the challenging times. If college degrees were easy to get, then EVERYONE would have one. This is far from reality in this country.

Let's talk a moment about what to do when your major gets hard. **"Switching majors" multiple times is similar to committing financial, chronological, and motivational suicide.** You don't have the money, the time, or the drive to switch majors like you switch your underwear. Listen, I know of many students who've told me that the only reason they switched majors was because the previous one got too hard. It became too intense, too difficult, and required too much study and work. **Well baby, news flash. LIFE IS THE EXACT SAME WAY.** Beyond college,

Delatorro L. McNeal II 65.

Major Selection Success

things don't get easier - they get more challenging. However, there's hope because the **REWARDS get much sweeter as well.** So, do your big brother a favor. Take a deep breath for me and decide right now that you are not going to be tossed to and fro by the winds of "switching majors" multiple times. It's just not smart and you are much too focused and determined to allow that to happen.

Lastly, remember this. **DON'T BE RULED BY HOW YOU FEEL.** This entire world is run by people who don't feel like it. Do you think Oprah always feels like being on camera? Do you think Mel Gibson always feels like acting or directing? Do you think I always feel like speaking or writing? NO! **But you do what you have to do, till you get to do what you want to do.** Push past how you feel, and begin to focus on what you KNOW you need to do to be successful.

Notes:

_____

_____

_____

_____

_____

_____

Rule #3

Shadow professionals who do what you want to do!

One of the things that makes college easier and harder at the same time is when you can shorten the "long-term" feeling that says, "One day I will be doing this, making this money, and living this way!" **You, my friend, have to power to collapse time and get sneak previews of the type of life you will be able to live beyond college. You can do this by surrounding yourself with people who are already doing what you want to ultimately do in life.** The reason why I say that this rule makes college easier and harder is because these types of people, (mentors and coaches) will cut years off your learning curve, which will make college easier for you. **Simultaneously, they will also demand so much more from you than anyone else in your life because they see the greatness within you and will not allow you to settle for a mediocre college experience.** Thus, they will make your life more challenging. They will not put up with excuses, nor will they settle for average grades and half-done projects.

If you really want to get the most out of college, find people who are already majoring in what you want to major in and become friends with them. Ask them which professors to take and which ones to avoid. To take it a step further, try to find people who have already graduated with the same degree you are trying to earn. On a college campus, you will find many of these types of people in Adjunct Professor positions. Ask these people to give you a "Day in the Life" example of what they do with their major and the degree that you hope to earn. Ask to shadow them for a day. You could follow them around and help them do what they do so you can LEARN FIRST HAND what it takes to be successful in your near future.

When I was in grad school, I got an internship with a company called W.D. Dick and Associates. The CEO's name was David Dick and he owned his own consulting business. I worked as an Instructional Systems Design (ISD) intern for 1 full year. Not only did I learn a great deal about the ISD field as a professional, but I also learned how to run my own business. David mentored me while I was still in my major program of study. I owe a portion of my present success to what he taught me then. You can experience the same thing. **Just seek out people who have been there and done that because they will help you Go There and Do That!**

Notes:

_____

_____

_____

_____

_____

_____

_____

Rule #4

Pick jobs, internships, and careers aligned with your Major!

The department from which you are earning your degree should be regularly inviting companies, organizations, and groups to present to you on exactly what they are looking for when they interview. **ATTEND as many of these functions as possible.** They will cut your learning curve by showing you all the answers to the test months, sometimes years, before you take it. Get it! So, if ABC Company sponsors a lunch-and-learn activity in your college, GO. Sit up front. Get there early and help set up. Stay afterwards and help clean up. **Pick the brains of the people who are there because they are doing what you ultimately want to do.** They can help you demystify your expectations by helping you to push past the promises of a glossy brochure and learn the realities of doing the work in the industry. You want and need to get this type of information.

To make your major really come alive and not seem boring or monotonous, **you must mix up your class-going with activities that allow you to use what you have learned in a fun and interactive way.** Try to find work-study opportunities that will force you to be mentored or supervised by someone within your major. Basically, you want to immerse yourself with people who are out there doing it.

I think the following analogy will help you understand what I mean. You have an appointment to graduate from college one day. You have a set appointment, time, and date when you will walk proudly and boldly across the stage of sacrifice and into the exciting world of possibility and destiny. Now, as long as your steps in college are aligned properly with that

Major Selection Success

appointment, you will not miss it. **However, the moment you take on a job or position that is not in alignment with your graduation, you get off track or misaligned from your goal. The result is that you end up feeling DIS-appointed. The feeling of disappointment is a result of you taking an action that pulls you away from your appointment with your destiny.** Now please understand, I am not at all saying that you should not work a job to get bills paid, even though that job is not in line with your major. What I am saying is that you should always have the larger goal in mind and don't allow yourself to be off-track for a prolonged amount of time. I hope you can understand that. So, what I want you to do is ask your Advisory Board to stay on the lookout for great job, internship, and career opportunities for you that will supplement your classroom experience.

Notes:

_____

_____

_____

_____

_____

_____

Chapter 6

Time Investment Success

Rule #1

Get a planner/organizer and USE IT DAILY!

Let me ask you a question my friend. What is the purpose of a bank account? No really…think about it for a moment. What is the real purpose of having and using a bank account? The answer is that a bank account gives you a safe place to store your money, manage credits & debits, and determine when you have enough money to do what you need to do. Well, just as a bank account does all these things for your money, a planner/organizer does the exact same things for your time. **YOU CAN'T MANAGE YOUR TIME EFFECTIVELY IF YOU DON'T HAVE A SYSTEM THAT SHOWS YOU WHERE YOUR TIME IS STORED.** I know plenty of students who want to be successful and get their lives on the right track. Unfortunately, many of these students don't have a clue as to how they will get started because they waste so much time.

You need to start telling your time where to go, instead of asking it where it went. In order to tell your time where to go, you must open a time account. Let me ask you a quick question. Are you more technology-oriented or are you more tactile-oriented? Tactile people prefer to write things down and manage their time with paper planners, calendars, and post-it notes. Technology people prefer to use Outlook, Lotus Notes, PDAs, and other digital devices to manage their time. Either way, choose which method you prefer and begin using an organizer to keep your life on track. My good friend Tony McGee, a professional speaker and author based in Los Angeles, says, **"Time is not money, because you can always earn back money".** For example, if you blow $10 dollars, you can earn $10

Time Investment Success

back. However, if you blow 10 minutes, you can never get those 10 minutes back because in life there are no rewind buttons, except those that exist within our minds.

One last thing. You will never HAVE TIME for anything in life. You must learn how to MAKE TIME. Don't fall into the familiar trap of feeling as though you're a victim to a lack of time in your day. No…No…No! You create the time you need in your day to do what needs to be done. Remember, stop asking your time where it went, and start telling your time where to go!

Notes:

_____

_____

_____

_____

_____

_____

_____

_____

Rule #2

Create a daily success routine!

I love this rule! One of the most important success principles of life is about to be revealed to you right now! Ready? Dr. Mike Murdock says,

"THE SECRET TO YOUR SUCCESS LIES IN WHAT YOU DO DAILY."

My friend, if you can learn this principle while in college, you will be massively successful. **The absolute secret to all success is hidden within the daily routine of a person.** I can dissect your daily routine and determine whether you will succeed or fail at a goal that you have set for yourself. If someone is very successful, their success can be traced back to something they did consistently. If someone is a failure in life, their failure can be traced back to something they did on a consistent, daily basis. Michael Jordan - who used to shoot over 300 jump shots EACH DAY - is very successful. Why? Well, this is because he was willing to do, daily, what most other players were not willing to do.

"THE SUCCESSFUL DO WHAT THE UNSUCCESSFUL FAIL TO DO!"

Therefore, since you are a successful student, I want to quickly share with you some things that you must do in order to create a daily success routine. By implementing each of the following tasks into each day you live and breathe, you will be very successful with the goals you have set.

1. Each morning, before you do anything major, **create a To-Do List.** This is a simple listing of things that you want

Delatorro L. McNeal II

Time Investment Success

to accomplish before you lay your head back on your pillow at night. Create a list of 8 things that you must do within your day, work from that list, and carry it with you.

2. Create time for academic, social, personal, physical, and spiritual growth. **Review your notes** for the class you will have that day for at least 10 minutes. Go with a friend to the gym to combine your social and physical well-being. **Read or listen to something that is spiritually motivating.**

3. **Post and Review your goals** for the week, everyday. Keep them fresh in your mind and take 10 minutes, each day, to strategize and organize for the next day and week to come. Planning for 10 minutes saves you 5 hours of time later on. Go for it!

Notes: _____

_____

_____

_____

_____

_____

_____

Delatorro L. McNeal II

Rule #3

Master your energy cycle!

We all have a time when we are at our best each day. Additionally, we also have a time when we are at our worst each day. **It is very important that you know yourself well enough to recognize when your energy cycle is at its best, and when your energy cycle is at its worst.** I am sure you have heard a lot of people say that they are "a morning person" or "a late-night person". Well, these people are basically sharing with you their personal energy cycles. In order to get the most out of each one of your days, it is important that you understand which times of the day you are at your best mentally, emotionally, and physically. For example, if you are NOT a morning person, DON'T register your hard classes in the morning. *Why?* **Because you would be working AGAINST your own energy cycle.** You are basically asking for trouble. Smiles… Instead, if you absolutely have to take morning classes, put your easier subjects - not requiring as much brainpower - in the morning. Then, take your more challenging classes later in the day. Remember, you are in college. YOU have the power to CREATE your schedule. Gone are the high school days of having to go to periods that are pre-assigned to you. NO…you can pick and choose and customize.

Here's another great tip. Don't go to class everyday if you don't have to. *Why?* You must be wise about how you create your schedule. Work with your energy cycle. If you like having 4-day weekends, then register for ALL Tuesday/Thursday classes. Now understand, you will have to work your butt off on those days off from class by disciplining yourself to study. However, you will also have

Time Investment Success

more time to work a part-time or full-time job, depending on your circumstance. Saturday classes are becoming more popular in colleges because these classes bring a more relaxed atmosphere than your typical weekday classes. You have a lot of options in college, so use your power to create a weekly routine that frees you up to embrace the other facets of your college experience.

To conclude, it does not matter whether you're a morning, afternoon, or evening person. What matters is that you know the type of person you are and understand that you have the power to customize your life, so it will systematically align with your body's natural physiology.

Notes: _____

_____

_____

_____

_____

_____

_____

_____

Rule #4

Discover what your time is worth!

You will never be able to accurately determine if your time is being wasted until you know how much your time is worth. **Additionally, until you know what your time is worth, you don't really know what or who you DO and DON'T have time for. There should be certain things that you don't have time for** - such as childish games, rumors, gossip, beating around the bush, jealously, and the list goes on. Similarly, there should be certain individuals that you don't have time for, such as back-biters, gossipers, playa haters, negative folks, and folk that are going absolutely nowhere. Remember this one rule about people. People are just like elevators - they either take you UP or they take you DOWN. It's that simple. So, make sure that you are always on the elevator ride heading in the upward direction.

The only real way to understand what and who you do and don't have time for is to measure how much your time is actually worth. I will use myself as an example. In 2003, corporations paid me $3,500 per hour for my time to speak, coach, and consult with their employees. Now, it would be insane for me to waste my time with negative people who are not going anywhere or negative money-making schemes that do the same – especially when I KNOW that my time is worth 3K and above. So, I don't hold conversations with people unless I see gold in them. I only interact with, mentor, and advise people who I believe will show a return on my investment through their action taken towards their greatness. If I see gold in you - I will stop and talk with you. Now, that is not snobbish because I see GOLD in homeless people. I see GOLD in restaurant waitresses. I see GOLD in almost

Time Investment Success

Delatorro L. McNeal II

everyone, but I also can tell when someone is trying to waste my time. When I perceive that, I quickly limit my interaction with them. I want you to learn to do the same. So, let's say that while in college, you are earning $18,000 a year. One hour of your time is worth $9.22. So, the next time your crazy girlfriend or boyfriend is coming to you with drama, be a good friend, but don't hang out long because your time is worth something very special. You must give your time to places and people who will give you a positive return on your investment. **Think investment when it comes to your time!**

Notes:

_____

_____

_____

_____

_____

_____

_____

_____

Delatorro L. McNeal II

Plan for success... or plan for failure!

Success is not Automatic...it is VERY Manual. People are not accidentally successful. The people who do become accidentally successful also end up losing what they had, almost as quickly as they got it. You must plan to be successful by making a conscious effort to decide that you WILL succeed. You WILL succeed by any positive means necessary. I know many students who think that once they get their college degree, success will automatically come their way. Sorry...it doesn't work that way. People that are TRULY successful in business, in family, in spirit, in body, in emotions, and in finances do things on purpose. They plan to be successful because they know that nothing comes to a sleeper but a dream. A professional speaker, trainer, and author who is also one of my mentors and dear friends, Tye Maner, often says something I love. He says, *"Good things do come to those who wait, but only those things left behind by those who Hustle!"* I love that quote because it speaks to the fact that we must be purposeful in our actions towards success in college and in life. A current U.S. statistic indicates that **95% of people who win the lottery (automatic success) will go BANKRUNPT in 3 to 5 years.** They achieve the goal of unlimited financial wealth and abundance; however, they ultimately end up failing. Why is this? Well, this is because TRUE SUCCESS is manual - it takes a process and a strategy. Anytime you acquire something without a process and strategy that teaches you along the way, you end up attaining something that you can't maintain because **you never developed into the right type of person in the process.** That is why having clearly defined, specific, and purpose-driven GOALS are so important to every college student's life and success. So, since we are planning to succeed, let me share 3 quick tips about your goals.

Time Investment Success

Delatorro L. McNeal II

1. You are never working on a goal. **A goal is always working on you.** It is always trying to turn you into a better person in the process.

2. The achievement of your goal is not as important as **WHO you BECOME in the process.** What do you want your goals to make you? More focused? More productive? A better judge of character?

3. Goals are not things you set in January or at the beginning of the Fall or Spring. **Goals are a part of you.** You work towards them all the time. Treat them like family because they will reward you when you do.

Notes:

_____

_____

_____

_____

_____

_____

_____

_____

Chapter 7
Motivation &
Empowerment Success

Rule #1

Understand that Knowledge is not Power; Applied Knowledge is Power!

All of your life you have been taught that knowledge is power. This would mean that the more you know the more you grow. Additionally, this would mean that new information automatically leads to new transformation. **Both of these are false.** We now live in the information age. Through the Internet, information or data is readily available to the rich just as easily as it is available to the poor. So, everyone has access to information/knowledge, yet everyone is not successful. Why is that? Why isn't everyone successful? Why is it that everyone has access to the same stock market information, but most of the wealth in this country is owned by 1% of the population? I'll tell you why. **This happens because knowledge, in and of itself, IS NOT POWER.** Information and data is not power. The ONLY WAY that knowledge, information, and data become power is when it is APPLIED. The entrepreneur, speaker, author, and pastor, Robert Mallan, often says, **"Information without Application leads to Frustration!"** That is SO TRUE. If you know something, but you don't apply what you know to a situation, you will end up mad at yourself for not using the knowledge that you had in a more productive way.

College forces you to read, write, and apply what you learn. The funny thing is that most students hate tests, exams, and projects, which are opportunities for you to APPLY what you know. If this is the case, then why do we hate tests and exams so much? It is because we are raised to be information junkies without being application addicts. We are raised to be inundated by television, movies, magazines, email, and the Internet — **NONE OF WHICH really challenge**

Motivation & Empowerment

us to APPLY what we know, ONLY ABSORB it. Some people say that the more you learn, the more you earn. They pursue advanced degrees just to say that they learned more, with ultimate hopes of earning more. Well, the reality is that the average self-made millionaire in this country only holds a 2.8 GPA. **This means that it is not what you learn (major) or how well you learn it (grade). Instead, it is how you APPLY what you've learned to your daily life (implementation) that makes you successful.** Start applying what you know, and you will be amazed at the results you get.

Notes:

_____

_____

_____

_____

_____

_____

_____

_____

Rule #2

Push past the Pain of Boredom and Blend your Day!

This rule is especially for my incoming freshman and transfer students. There will come a time when the newness of the college experience and the "honeymoon" period of being away from home and on your own will wear off. There will come a time when going to classes, seeing cute guys and fine girls, attending football games, and going clubbin' on Friday night won't excite you anymore. When that revelation comes, there is one thing I can say to sum up my advice to you.

WELCOME TO THE REAL WORLD OF COLLEGE LIFE.

The glitz and glamour of college is great, but it is just like a vapor - here one minute and gone the next. Football season is here one minute and gone the next. Pretty women are a dime a dozen. Fine guys are in every class. Once you've been to one club, you have been to them all. So, what else is there? **There's LIFE. You see, all those other things are temporary motivators. They are good for a season - a very brief season - and afterwards you must find something else to stimulate your passion.** When all the newness wears off and you realize that you still have 2 to 4 years to get this thing called college right, it becomes a brand new ball game. So, what do you do when going to class is no longer fun or enjoyable? What do you do when you find yourself skipping class? What do you do when you feel like cheating on a test, just to prevent studying for it?

STOP THE MADNESS AND REMEMBER WHY YOU ARE HERE.

Motivation & Empowerment

Delatorro L. McNeal II   87.

Skipping class does not hurt the professor…it hurts YOU. Cheating on a test, when you're supposed to be applying your knowledge, does not hurt the instructor…it hurts YOU. Stop all the boring talk about college. Every student has an "I hate my boring professor" story. Instead of complaining, start blending your day. **In other words, put exciting extracurricular activities on the same day of your boring classes. Also, put something fun before and after your boring classes to keep you motivated to perform well and enjoy the rest of your day.** Don't allow anything to stop you from getting everything you can from your college experience.

Notes:

_____

_____

_____

_____

_____

_____

_____

_____

Develop an unstoppable positive attitude!

The **#1 thing that separates the good from the great, the ordinary from the extraordinary, and the poor from the wealthy is one word that has tremendous meaning: ATTITUDE.** We hear this word ALL THE TIME, but I believe that most people never really understand what it means and how critical it is for achieving and maintaining success.

If you are going to achieve anything of real significance in college and beyond, you must learn how to develop and maintain an **UNSTOPPABLE, positive, and winning attitude about life. The reality is that you can earn a 4.0 GPA in college, have a "jacked up" attitude, and do nothing with your degree.** This happens all the time! You can also have a 3.6 GPA and a winning attitude, which allows you to out-perform, out-interview, out-earn, and out-execute those with higher GPAs. I love the way Joe Martin says, **"It's not about your IQ. It's about your I WILL."** This simply means that you must decide within yourself that you will have a positive outlook on your life, your circumstances, your challenges, your victories, your struggles, and your successes. Now, just because you are positive does not mean that things will always go your way. In fact, many times they won't. However, I believe that you can't always control what happens TO YOU, but you certainly can control what happens IN YOU.

Decide, today, that you will look at life through the proper lenses. You will look at life through the "glasses of greatness." You will intentionally look for the greatness in others. You will intentionally give

Delatorro L. McNeal II

people the benefit of the doubt. **You will realize and understand that "the rest of your life is the best of your life" and the greatest of times are NOT behind you — they are ahead of you.** There are several easy and fun ways to ensure that you maintain a positive attitude on a daily basis. **First, listen to something positive the first 20 minutes and the last 20 minutes of your day.** Protect how your day starts and ends, by giving yourself something positive to meditate on. **Second, surround yourself with positive friends and associates. You will become whom you associate with, so choose wisely. Third, read one positive, motivational book each month. Your input really and truly does determine your output.** Remember, how you FEEL about something is within YOUR control. **Decide to be victor in life, not a victim.** Also, remember that your attitude will determine your altitude!

Notes: _____

_____

_____

_____

_____

_____

Rule #4

Learn from Everything!

I am sure that over the many years you have been in school, you have heard of the Law of Cause and Effect. Well, in this rule, I want to focus on the fact that each effect in life produces something called a RESULT. **Everything you do in life, everyday, is producing some type of result for you. It may not always be getting you closer to the goal, but it is producing a result.** Every note you take in class produces a result in your memory, test-taking skills, and comprehension of the material. Every conversation you have with someone you're interested in dating produces a result - it either draws you closer to that person or drives you further away. Everything you purchase produces a result. *What's the point?* I am so glad you asked! If everything you do in life is going to produce a result, then it is "mission critical" that you begin to do two things with the results you get.

1. **Learn from every result you get.** This includes the bad results. These are even the results that were embarrassing and humiliating. Also, these are the results that you haven't told anyone about. LEARN SOMETHING FROM THEM.

2. **Once you have learned something from your result, APPLY that knowledge the next time a similar situation arises,** so that you can handle it better.

Life is nothing but a BIG classroom. I believe that Life and God are always trying to TEACH us something. If we fail to learn from the mistakes we make in life, we will also fail future tests and have to repeat that "class" ALL OVER AGAIN. Let me give you an example. Have you

Motivation & Empowerment

ever dated someone and, after a few months, realized that this person is just like the previous person you broke-up with? It almost seems as if you were dating the same person with the exception of a different name and face. Well, that could be due to the fact that you did not change your dating criteria BEFORE you selected your new mate. My dear friend and fellow speaker, Jonathan Sprinkles, often says, **"In order to change the mate, first change the BAIT."** Change what you are using to "hook" the person. If you want better results in life, you must begin by LEARNING FROM your experiences and APPLYING what you have learned to get better, more productive, and more successful results in the future. Life is a teacher!

Notes:

_____

_____

_____

_____

_____

_____

_____

_____

Rule #5

Don't rely solely on your talent!

This rule is so important. I am about to say something that is rather paradoxical, but I promise that you will understand it by the end of my explanation.

TALENT MATTERS, BUT AT THE SAME TIME - IT DOESN'T!

This rule is so important because I know people who spend their entire lives trying to become the most talented person in their field of study. Now, that is a very wise and intelligent thing to do, and I recommend that you work as hard as you can to be as proficient at your gifts as possible. **However, it is not the people with the most talent who are the most successful in life.** Try turning on the radio or the TV some day. I mean…really. Have you ever been listening to a singer, band, or radio host and wondered how in the world they got a record deal? I know I have! Have you ever watched a movie that was so horrible that you wanted a refund after it was over? Again, I know I have. Regardless of what you and I thought about the movie, song, TV show, or radio program, the person still was in a position of maximum exposure of their gifts and talents, even though their talents weren't that great. **The reality is that there will always be someone out there who is MORE talented than you.** So, in the game of life, it's not about who is the most talented. Life is about **who can EXPOSE their talent in the marketplace**, so people will know about them and create opportunities.

Don't solely rely on your degree to make you successful. Don't expect your parents' connections or your school's

Motivation & Empowerment

credibility, alone, to get you in the door. **Work on mastering your gift as much as you can, while simultaneously working on getting yourself exposed to the people who can appreciate your talent and help you get it polished and packaged for the marketplace.** If you can sing, dance, write, read, act, cook, design, produce, build, administrate, organize, fundraise, govern, lead, protect, emcee, speak, orchestrate, play, edit, capture, operate, defend, create, innovate, or whatever…DO WHAT YOU DO, and do it so people can see it. When your season comes — and it will — you will be ready to soar with the best of them. I believe in you, my friend. Get your talents exposed!

Delatorro L. McNeal II

Rule #6

Move from decision to regular intelligent action!

The college experience greatly deals with one word: **SEARCHING.** Everyone in college is searching for a variety of things. People are searching for meaning, belonging, mates, significance, success, living space, majors, careers, employment, mentors, love, spiritual growth and development, purpose and passion in life, and so forth. The search is on, and many people search without finding. Others search and don't like what they find. So, to help empower you to be a student and world-changer that is different from the rest, I have created this rule.

Searching is good and necessary for a season, but searching is also VERY expensive. This expense can include money, as well as emotions, time, peace, joy, and contentment in life. **I want to shift you from being a college student who is always searching - to a college student who is DECISIVE.** One of the greatest characteristics of GREAT people is that most great people are very decisive. They don't take all day to decide on something. **Instead of aimlessly searching, they deliberately RESEARCH and find the evidence necessary to move forward in a direction that is productive and profitable.** I believe, without question, that your destiny is shaped by the decisions you make in life. In addition, I believe the quality of your decisions determine the quality of your life. So, if you want a better life, start making better and more informed decisions.

Now that I have said that, let me take you deeper to help you understand that making a decision IS NOT enough. **Once you make a decision, you must ACT on what you decide and consistently move forward.** For

Motivation & Empowerment

Delatorro L. McNeal II

95.

example, 3 frogs are sitting by a still pond, and 1 decides to jump. How many are left? There should be 2 frogs now, right? Nope, 3 are left because the 1 frog just decided!

Make the decision to be a decisive person, and then move forward by becoming a person of action. Once you start taking action, make sure you are consistent. You will quickly learn just how powerful of an individual you really are. Go for it!

Notes: _____

_____

_____

_____

_____

_____

_____

_____

Learn when to break the rules & create new ones!

I love this rule. I believe that you will too. **Sometimes in life, you must decide to break the rules. There will be times in your college experience when doing things the "same ole way" won't work anymore.** There will be times when your passion for something will boil so much that you may act in a way that is not in line with the existing policies and procedures of an organization. **When this happens, it is important to keep the main thing, the main thing.** Also, remember the "WHY" in your life. Let me explain. If you have never seen the movie, *Men of Honor*, then you MUST see and buy this movie, and add it to your motivational collection. In this movie, Carl Brushier - played by Cuba Gooding, Jr. - is a young African American man who aspires to become a Navy Master Diver during a time when blacks were not "allowed" to achieve that goal. Great story short, he ends up bending and breaking all the racist rules that were put into place to hold him back, and he used his life story to set new rules and create standards of success. Just as that time came for Carl to break the rules, the time will also come in your life when you must break the rules to follow your purpose and passion to attain success.

The time will come when you will have to lean on the strength of your reasons for why something is right and stand up for it. **You must remember that right is right, even if no one is for it, and wrong is wrong even when everyone is for it.** Please remember that. It may be standing up for poor or disadvantaged students who can't stand up for themselves. It may be creating policies in student government for a minority group that is drastically underrepresented. It may be ratting out a "friend" of yours

Motivation & Empowerment

who mistreated a person of the opposite sex in a court case. It may be standing up for your spiritual beliefs in the midst of a campus wide revolt. You never know what will happen. However, one thing you should know is that **YOU HAVE THE POWER to STAND UP** for what you believe in and let your voice be heard. Do you know the old saying "rules are meant to be broken?" Well, I say that rules are only meant to be broken when a better and more successful rule can take its place. Since this book is called "Rules of the Game," I want you to take a quick break from reading and write down a few of your own rules that you have learned from family, friends, or relatives, and would like to apply in college.

Notes: _____

_____

_____

_____

_____

_____

_____

Delatorro L. McNeal II

Chapter 8
Family Success

Hold On and Let Go!

Dealing with family while in college and matriculating through college is a degree program in and of itself! There are so many different facets of the familial relationship that must be considered and properly balanced in order to maintain your sanity. People are raised differently, so this chapter of rules will probably be very different from the others. The word family, to most people, means mother, father, sister, brother, and other close relatives. This is a correct and appropriate definition. However, there are also many people who don't have the benefit of knowing who their birth mother or father is. Additionally, the rise of single-parent families in our nation has made it more popular to call people "family" when there is no blood connection. In fact, you could have a next-door neighbor who served as a big brother to you for years. Therefore, you may consider that person to be closer to you than a blood relative.

Regardless of how you define family or who fits into your definition of family, while in college it is important that you hold on to the people that love and support you. Additionally, you must let go a little. Expect things to be different in college. Expect to be home sick for a small period of time. It's normal. Also expect to meet new people, experience new perspectives, and embrace new friendships that could potentially last a lifetime. I read a quote one time that I love. It says, ***"You will never discover new oceans, until you have the courage to lose sight of the shore!"*** This means that we get so comfortable with those we are close to that we expect them to ALWAYS be there for us. However, you must always have the faith to know that those you hold dear in life are not going anywhere simply because you are miles away at college. You must have the courage to shift your focus by faith, knowing that the safety of shore (home) is not changing just because you are looking at new possibilities and new directions of discovery (college). Get it? There is a world out there full of bad people and GREAT people. Discover the great ones, latch hold of them, and become great in the process. But most of all, remember that your family and close friends will always have your back during the process.

Notes:

_____

_____

_____

_____

_____

_____

_____

_____

Rule #2

Never burn your bridges!

Now, as a caveat to my last point, it is mission critical that you maintain open and positive relationships with the people who have loved and supported you over the years. I know a lot of students who go off to college or graduate school and start to totally "DIS" their family and close friends. This usually happens because they are pursuing degrees that no one else in their family has or because they have met the person they deem to be "Mr. or Mrs. Right." This is a wrong move that could cost you some really dear friendships and family relationships. **"Out of sight" does not have to mean "out of mind."** In fact, I believe that what you do when someone is not looking is more important than what you do while they are looking. This is an indication of what a person REALLY wants to do. A person's true motives are discovered when they take action in the absence of corrective words.

I know students who have had very successful dating relationships. They go off to college thinking that they have "arrived" and end up dissing the person back home. Then they find out that the person they tried to date on campus was playing them. So, they run back to the "home relationship" and find no one there because no one likes to be dissed! **Don't burn your bridges.** Now, I am not saying that you can't break up with a high school sweetheart if the relationship has gone bankrupt. If this is the case, I recommend that you end the relationship. However, don't dismiss people out of your life just because you think you are ALL THAT, when people who are close to you know that you're NOT. Don't burn your bridges.

Family Success

Don't believe all the hype. I know students who began to treat their loved ones like trash as they matriculated through college. They thought they had it all under control because they had their own job, apartment, and friends. They no longer felt that they needed mom's advice or dad's money, so they started to believe that life was great without them. Please my friend, get this rule in your head. **Every person in your life is a bridge. Each bridge in life helps you get from one point to another.** The ONLY bridges you ever need to burn in life are those with negative, toxic, and dangerous people connected to them. **All other bridges must stay in good condition, because you never know when you will need to use one of those same bridges to bring you to a place of comfort, support, love, and safety.** Treat people right! You need to celebrate those who've helped you to grow up, develop, learn, and overcome in life. Without these people, you would not be where you are today. We all are riding on the backs of other people who have helped to prepare the way for us. So, never give up and never lose sight of the "small" people who have helped to bring you to your present position of promise.

Notes:

_____

_____

_____

_____

Rule #3

Create extended family relationships!

We talked a little about this principle in Chapter 1 on Academic Success, but I would like to further explain it here, because it is so vitally important to understanding the role that positive people play in your life. **The college experience gives you a wonderful opportunity to create some AWESOME extended family relationships.** These are relationships with people who are not blood relatives, but who you bond with, due to the oneness of spirit, personality, and character you share. This bond is sometimes just as - or even more - powerful than your feeling of connectedness towards some blood relatives.

Now, please understand something. These relationships will not develop overnight - they will take some time. The wonderful thing is that when you find these people in your life, you will have found a goldmine of love and support that transcends time, space, age, gender, and socio-economic status. I would like to give you two examples of what I am talking about.

Omega Forbes is one of my best friends in the entire world. I met him in Tallahassee during my freshman year at Florida State. I had heard of him in the community because he is a National Gospel Recording Artist. We ended up singing next to each other when I joined the Collegiate Choir at Tabernacle M.B. Church. **Here's a quick note: It is very important that you find a place to feed your spiritual life while away from home.** Anyway, Omega and I met, clicked, and became dear friends. From that time until now, we have never argued about anything. Not to say that arguments are not healthy, but we have always had a divine

Family Success

understanding of each other. We depend and count on each other. I was one of his Best Men in his wedding and I am one of the God Parents to his beautiful daughter, Destiny. Also, his wife, Taneka, and my wife, Nova, are great friends. He is truly a brother to me and I love him dearly.

My second example comes in the form of one of my mentees, **Kyle Rodgers.** Currently, he is a student at the University of Central Florida. He is a powerful young person whose mission is to, *Empower a Now Generation for Takeover.* He is a powerful young speaker, Christian Rap Artist, and a Minister of Mime. I have learned so much from him, and I am blessed to teach him many great things about college and life in general. I do not have any "blood" younger brothers, but Kyle, without question, is a younger brother in my life. I love him dearly. Every time I talk with him, I see the years fall off of his learning curve, because as he continues to apply himself to his studies and dreams, he will surpass me in his accomplishments. His parents, Dwight and Jeanne Rodgers, are nationally recognized speakers, trainers, and authors in the area of Marriage & Family Empowerment. Kyle reminds me of myself – the young man I was in college. What's better about him is that he is WISER than I was 7 years ago.

My point in sharing these two stories with you is very critical. **There are people who will come into your life who don't look like you or come from your background, but they will be with you through hardships, challenges, and successes. They will hold you accountable to the true level of greatness you really** possess! I believe that God has a funny way of blessing us with the things we ask for and need. I have never had blood sisters, but through extended family I have about ten. I have extended brothers, sisters, moms, and dads and I NEED them all in a very special way. You will experience this same thing if you avail yourself to these types of wonderful relationships.

Notes:

_____

_____

_____

_____

_____

_____

_____

_____

Family Success

Notes:

_____

_____

_____

_____

_____

_____

_____

_____

_____

_____

_____

_____

_____

_____

_____

_____

_____

_____

_____

Rule #4

Go forth anyway - regardless of support!

Before, during, and after college, you will have many people promise you many things! In addition to many promises, there will be people who will say that you have their support. The funny thing is that when it really counts, their support will be absent. This is not negative - it's just the truth. Once you make the decision to **GROW THROUGH COLLEGE** and not just go to college, you must determine in your mind and heart that you will give college your best effort. Family is important, but you can't let family hold you back from pursuing the things that you know to be true. I can tell you many stories of students who went to college on the financial and emotional promises of others, only to arrive and discover that the support was not there. The reality is that you have begun something. Now, my question is, **"Will you finish it?"** My follow up question is, **"Will you finish it STRONG?"** You must, because your destiny is depending on you!

So they promised to help you with a car, rent, and food for the first 2 years. Now, they are coming up with excuses. **GO FORTH ANYWAY!**

So, they said they would be faithful to your dating relationship. Then you get a call and find out that they started cheating on you as soon as you left town. **GO FORTH ANYWAY!**

So they totally disagree with you following your heart to major in something that is not in the family tradition. **GO FORTH ANYWAY!**

Family Success

So they don't like the fact that you are dating interracially or interculturally. They seem to not answer the phone when you call or to not invite your significant other over for holidays because of blatant racism. Do me one favor, my friend. **GO FORTH ANYWAY!**

So they say you are important to them and they seem to make time to visit everyone else BUT you in college. Therefore, the only time they visit you in college is at graduation, where everyone assumes that they have been a supportive parent all along – and in your heart you know otherwise. In spite of all that - **GO FORTH ANYWAY!**

My friend, in spite of what people say to you, if you never give up, work your butt off, and stay focused on your dream and your inner source of strength, you will be successful. **You will be so successful that others will have to sit on the sidelines of your success to watch and deal with the reality that you did it WITHOUT THEM.** Others don't have to believe in your dream! As long as you believe and take action, the SKY is NOT the limit because there's NO LIMITS to what you can be or achieve.

MAKE IT...EVEN IF IT'S ON BROKEN PROMISES!

Notes:

_____

_____

Rule #6

Do it for you!

There is one person whose goals, dreams, aspirations, financial future, and destiny are riding on the residual results of your college experience -**YOU!** You must learn to do this FOR YOU! You are not in college to please your parents, professors, friends, someone you want to date, me, or some corporation. **DO IT FOR YOURSELF.** You are the pilot of your college flight, and you will continue to soar as long as your attitude stays high and positive. Don't let other people's expectations of the importance of college determine how seriously you take your own experience.

Determine that you are worth your weight in GOLD. Determine how much your life is worth. **Determine that you are the CEO of your own life.** When you know your position, you then know your potential in life. When you decide to skip class, you are slapping yourself and your future in the face – regardless of how "boring" the class is. **Don't try to do things just to fit into some else's version of reality. NO! You create your own version of reality by studying the truth. The truth that you know and intimately apply in life will be what sets you free.**

·**Pick challenging courses for you,** not for someone else.
·**Pick intelligent friends for you,** not for someone else.
·**Pick a great school for you,** not because family wants you to go there.
·**Pick motivating professors for you,** not because they are cute.
·**Pick the right decisions for you,** not because you want to appear to be someone you really are not.

Family Success

Go to college to create a better you - a more focused, determined, and committed YOU. If not, you will look back with regrets. Don't regret your experience, but don't go buck wild by trying everything under the sun either. **Everything that shines is not silver, and everything that glitters is not gold. Every girl in tight jeans is not wife material, and every guy with dimples and a cute goatee will not be there for you when you're mother is in the hospital.** Set yourself free from the negative opinions of mankind, and focus on being the best YOU that you can be! Don't Settle!

Notes:

_____

_____

_____

_____

_____

_____

_____

_____

Chapter 9
Roommate Success

Rule #1

Be proactive about selection and retention!

I had 2 roommates during my college experience. My first roommate was, of course, during my freshman year and my last roommate came during my last 2 years of college (including 1 semester of undergrad and 3 semesters of graduate school). They were cool. I learned a lot from them both. Based on what they told me, they also learned a great deal from me about life and success. I lived by myself during my sophomore and junior years of college. Of course, that was great. However, roommates can do 1 of 2 things to your college experience - **Enrich it or Imprison it!** Think about it. You spend at least 1/3 of everyday around this individual, sharing space, sharing resources, sharing groceries, sharing furniture, sharing air – sharing almost everything.

Therefore, the first rule I must share with you on how to achieve success with a roommate is to be as proactive in the "roommate selection process" as possible. If you can pick your roommate, then do that. At least you'll know, upfront, what you are dealing with. If you can't pick them, now-a-days on many campuses you can give a very detailed description of the type of person you are looking to room with. Listen, don't take this roommate selection thing lightly. **You have to sleep there, eat there, study there, talk to friends and family there, balance your finances there, write papers there, and the list goes on and on.** So, you NEED to be as active as you can in the process of picking your roommates and screening them whether you are living in a dorm, apartment, or house. You need to make sure that there is a positive match. **Being nonchalant about this process will indicate that you don't mind sentencing yourself to a lot of unnecessary drama.**

Roommate Success

Delatorro L. McNeal II   115.

My freshman roommate, Ben, came from the same high school as I did. In fact, Ben and I lived in the same area of town and had a singing group together in high school. Rooming with Ben, for the most part, was a good experience. It was also very challenging at times, but still good. He was into fraternities - I was not. He was into alcohol - I was not. I was into class - he was not. I was into church - he was not. However, Ben taught me how to play racquetball. Now, I am bad-to-the-bone in racquetball because we found something in common that we could share together. **Remember to be proactive** and you will experience success with your roommates in college and beyond.

Notes:

_____

_____

_____

_____

_____

_____

_____

_____

Rule #2

Don't just share space - share an understanding!

Once you have a roommate, it is critical that you make the very best of your close living quarters. In order to do this, you must come to some common levels of understanding. I believe that in all of life, reaching an understanding is one of the most important things a person can do. Therefore, when you get your roommate, there are certain things that you must come to an understanding about.

1. **Food.** Come to an understanding on how you all want to buy and handle the food that comes into your dwelling. Some people shop together, while others shop separately and put labels on everything. Either way is fine, as long as you agree on a standard way of doing things and govern yourselves accordingly.

2. **Money, Rent, and Bills.** As a team, you all must work together to decide how the rent/mortgage will be paid. If you stay in a dorm, this will not apply to you, but the rest sure does. I know people who've gotten evicted because the roommate did not pay their portion of the rent on time. So, come to a quick understanding on bills and utility payments.

3. **Company/Guests.** If your roommate has guests - YOU have guests. It is very important that you create a system where there is clear and honest communication about when company should be invited over and how long they should stay. This is vital in dorm rooms. On the other hand, these rules can be more relaxed in apartments with separate bedrooms.

4. **Entertainment.** Everybody has a home-theatre system with killer bass now-a-days. It is important that you set some ground rules for how loud music and movies should be played. This will ensure that you all can study and focus when needed. Also, you

Roommate Success

won't have to deal with the complaints of your neighbors and the possibility of being reported for disrupting them.

5. **Personal Belongings.** This is a big one. Once you get comfortable in a place, you tend to take things for granted. I have heard horror stories of roommates wearing each other's clothes (even underwear and bathing suits) without the other's permission. Please make sure that you get an understanding from your roommate about which types of clothes are sharable and which ones are off limits. No one is entitled to take possession of your belongings without your permission.

Basically, make sure that you don't just live with people, but that you build a relationship with your roommates. The goal is for them to really understand you, your values, and your perspectives about things – and vice versa. This is very important!

Notes: _____

_____

_____

_____

_____

_____

_____

Rule #3

Be a leader in your house!

One very valuable lesson that I learned a long time ago was that people follow your footsteps quicker than they follow your advice. **Talk is cheap these days. So, it is important that you become a leader in your dwelling place to enable your roommate to not just hear how serious you are about success, but to SEE it also.** Don't leave it up to your roommate to set the atmosphere for your home - you set it. Don't wait for your roommate to bring up tough issues that need to be discussed - you bring them up. Don't wait for your roommate to clean up before the room looks better - you clean it yourself. Lead by example in your house. This is so important. You can have a major impact on the life of your roommate by being a positive example. But also remember this, don't get taken advantage of either. **You can lead by example without being your roommate's "do-boy or do-girl".**

Listen to this. I told you earlier that Ben was into alcohol. He used to drink a lot in college. Now, I never blasted Ben for drinking. I would remind him that he had class the next day, that same day, or within the hour. However, I did not blast him for choosing to drink. I stopped him when he wanted to drive, but I did not make him feel like I was trying to be his dad by giving constant lectures about the challenges of drinking. He knew that stuff already. Instead, I led by example. For instance, we would go to some of the same parties and social functions, and he could not understand how I was the life of the party without having one drop of alcohol in my system. Why? Well, I didn't need it. **He learned from watching me that he did not**

Roommate Success

need to drink alcohol to have a great time. So, I was able to impact my roommate not by what I said, but by what I did.

Another example of this principle is when I lived in an apartment with my roommate, Mitch, while in graduate school. We shared almost everything, cooked together a lot, and had similar friends, which made our relationship cool. One thing that Mitch says that I taught him was how to keep pursuing his dreams no matter what. I attended grad school during a time when the college told me there was no money for me. **Regardless of the "bad news" about them not having money for me - I applied, got accepted, and started school anyway. Within a matter of weeks, I had 3 assistantships! Mitch, a tremendously gifted musician and choral director,** was struggling at that time with the motivation to finish school. I am happy to report that he is doing great now, and he says that much of his motivation to finish came from watching me first hand. My friend, you just never know who is watching and just how much of an impact you are having on their lives. So don't forget to lead by example and your roommates will see your efforts and hopefully follow suite.

Notes: _____

_____

_____

_____

Rule #4

Try to grow together, if not, GROW ALONE!

That last rule brings up another really good and final principle that relates to roommates. There will be many things about you and your roommate that are very different. Therefore, you need to find some things that you have in common with one another. **Try to come up with activities that you can do jointly to promote the relationship, fun, educational growth, and professional development.** So, if you hear about a great speaker, seminar, or workshop coming to town, let your roommate know and encourage them to come with you. If you know of a great concert that is playing on campus, give your roomie a ring and see if they want to attend. Now, all of this is assuming that you like your roomie and enjoy spending some quality time with them. If not, go back to rule #1 in this chapter and see how you can be proactive about selecting your next roommate. Smiles…

Intentionally try to find areas that your roommate needs development in and try to invite them to events that stimulate that part of their growth. For example, if they are bad with time management, ask them to come with you to a seminar. If they hate studying, invite them to come to a cool study session that you enjoy. Please do the same for yourself. If you hate to do something that they do well, but you know you need to learn to do it, ask them to bring you along for things that will challenge you to grow. I believe that if you sow good intentions, you will reap good intentions. **I also believe that if you help to carry someone else who is weak in a certain area, they will, someday, help to carry you when you are weak.** I like to call this the Boomerang Effect.

Roommate Success

Lastly, **IF your roommate does not want to grow or develop, and go to the new levels that you are - GO ALONE!** Don't let anyone or anything hold you back from getting every positive thing that life has to offer you. **Work as diligently as you can to make your dreams come true and don't worry if others don't believe that it can happen for you. You believe in your dreams for yourself.**

Grow no matter what!
Grow if nobody supports you.
Grow if you have to study by yourself.
Grow if your roommate hates you.
Grow if you don't have a car yet.
Grow if you can't stand your professors.
Grow if people are talking about you.
Grow if people don't like your fashion sense.

Grow if you have to grow by yourself. If you are willing to grow, there is no limit to where you can GO!
God Bless.

Notes:

_____

_____

_____

_____

Chapter 10
Leadership Success

Rule #1

Lead without a Title - Just do it!

Leadership IS NOT a TITLE, a BADGE, or a POSITION. Leadership, as Dr. John Maxwell states, is "Influence". Now, the reality is this. You can lead someone to do good or you can lead someone to do bad. Why? Because the essence of leadership is simply influence. Therefore, everyone has the capacity to be a leader, because we all have the ability to influence someone at some point in our lives. Leadership is not about a title or a position - it is about the ability to influence someone or something. **Therefore, it becomes paramount that we learn how to lead without a name badge.** It becomes mission critical that we lead without people telling us to do so. It becomes vital that we lead…without a title. **Listen, my friend. You don't need a corner office, a fancy jacket, letters behind your name, your own website, a nice car, or a gated community to be a leader.** There is only 1 key ingredient that you need in order to qualify you as a candidate to be a great leader. Wanna know what that one ingredient is? Here it goes.

You must have The WILLINGNESS to influence someone or something for the better.

That is it. If you are not just able, but willing to do what it takes to positively influence someone or something and make it or them better - you qualify! CONGRATULATIONS! Now, my challenge to you is simple. **Lead** while no one is looking. **Lead** when no one is patting you on the back. **Lead** in your organizations when you are not the one sitting at the head table. **Lead** when you are not the one who is most popular. **Lead** when no one even knows your name. *Well*

Delatorro L. McNeal II   125.

Del, how do I do that? That's a Great Question. **Speak** your mind and share your thoughts and ideas in a positive and constructive way. **Listen** to the opinions and insights of others and encourage positive energy while amongst the team. **Recognize** when it's time to refocus and regroup. **Understand** when others disagree with your rationale. **Encourage** everyone in your group to participate. **Appreciate** people's efforts. Simply do all you can to create an environment that is positive and supports productivity, **and do it as a "nobody". Eventually, somebody will see it and, ultimately, everybody will celebrate it.**

Notes:

_____

_____

_____

_____

_____

_____

_____

Rule #2

Lead with a purpose!

True leaders understand their purpose. **True leaders understand the REASON behind why they do what they do.** One of the rules of being a great leader in college and beyond is being clear about the purpose of your leadership position, the role you play in the big picture, and the overall purpose of the organization. **Real leaders** understand that people don't work for them. **Genuine leaders** know that they work for people. **An honest leader** is not at the top of the organizational chart looking down at other people. Rather, he or she is at the bottom of the organizational chart, pushing other people up. **A synergistic leader** knows that his or her idea, alone, is nothing without the input of those who co-labor in the organization.

One of the biggest and most simple questions the human mind often asks us is "Why?" The ability for you to clearly and concisely answer this question when it arises determines how far from the path of simple knowledge and how close to the destination of profound wisdom you have really come. People always want to know why. People always ask purpose questions. **In order to be a powerful student leader, collegiate leader, and professional leader, you must clearly understand purpose.** You must understand the purpose of why you meet on the days and at the times you meet. You must understand the purpose behind your organizational structure. You must understand the purpose of why dues are what they are. You must also understand the purpose behind fundraisers, social functions, community service, business meetings, and the like. These must be CLEAR to the leadership before they will ever be understood, internalized, and externally manifested, which brings about true progress within the organization.

The leader has the vision of the organization. The leader clearly understands that, in order to possess the vision of tomorrow, specific, diligent, determined, and purpose-driven action steps must be taken TODAY. When the purpose of a thing is unknown, the abuse of that thing is guaranteed. **However, when the purpose of a thing is known, the optimization of that thing is also guaranteed.** So, as a leader - which you are - decide to begin to operate within the purpose of your leadership and the purpose of your organization. You will experience much success -not only now - but in the many years to come.

Notes:

_____

_____

_____

_____

_____

_____

_____

_____

Delatorro L. McNeal II

Rule #3

Lead with an agenda and a strategy!

As a leader, you must make sure that you have a plan when conducting important meetings in school, in business, and in your personal life. **Remember, if you fail to plan, then you are planning to fail.** When your study teams meet, there should be a plan in place as to what you are going to do with your time. This will enable the team to be as productive as possible, while having an enjoyable time learning and growing together. To this end, another great rule of being a great student leader and life leader is to lead with an agenda and a strategy. **An agenda is two things. First, an agenda is a listing of tasks, assignments, notes, topics, and action items that need to be discussed, delegated, and initiated during the course of your meeting. Second, an agenda is a motive that you have or a real intention that you have towards something or someone.** So as a leader, it is important that you take a proactive role and come to the meeting with your agenda written down with copies made for everyone involved. In addition to having items to discuss and delegate, there should also be a timeline set aside for the discussion of the items. Without a timeline, you could end up talking for much too long about one topic.

In addition to having a written outline of what needs to be covered, you must also be clear in your mind and heart about what you are trying to accomplish in and through the meeting. When people come to a meeting with multiple motives or what is commonly called "ulterior motives", conflict is inevitable. You as the leader must have the vision for the organization and impart that vision to everyone that works with you. If

Leadership Success

Delatorro L. McNeal II

129.

you're unable to impart the vision, you will then have more than one vision in the camp. **This ultimately creates "di-" (two or more) "vision" within your organization.** Lead your organization with a written plan that has an overarching vision/mission statement that everyone can work towards. Ensure, through clear communication and discussion, that everyone in your leadership team and everyone that is a part of your organization has the right motives in mind when they engage in any activities representative of the group. Do these simple, yet critical things, and you will experience repeated success as a leader in college and beyond.

Notes: _____

_____

_____

_____

_____

_____

_____

_____

Rule #4

Lead without letting "leadership" lead you!

Just because you are the leader by title and by experience doesn't mean that you have to know and do everything. Just because you are the head person in charge doesn't mean that you can or should talk to people any kind of way. Just because you have the office space and the business cards that let everyone in your organization know that you are the leader, does not mean that you are always right and that your way is the best way.

It is important that you understand that, as a leader, you don't have to possess all the knowledge and have all the answers to every situation. That is why you should have a team of people, like an executive board, who have your vision, but also think a little differently than you do. This will help the organization to benefit from the *synergy* that is created when like minds come together. I know students who had many friends when they were not in a leadership position. However, as soon as they got a little power, they let it go to their heads. As a result, they had to lead alone because they dissed all their friends for the sake of the position. Listen, I believe that it is very important that you keep negative people as far from your life as possible. **I also believe that you should keep positive people as close to your life as possible.** Having said that, know that you don't have to change your personality to be a great leader. **You can be an awesome leader and still be a little silly, still make people laugh, and still touch peoples' hearts all at the same time.** Learn how to lead without letting "leadership" lead you. If you're not careful, you will alienate people who really love you because you are trying to win the SGA President spot (for

Delatorro L. McNeal II

example). I know many people who have climbed the ladder of student government, while stepping over those they "loved" in the process. **They got to the top only to realize that it is very lonely at the top of "Success Mountain" when you have cheated and mistreated people to get there.**

Be smart...you AWESOME STUDENT LEADER, YOU. Encourage. Support. Motivate. Empower. Equip. Educate. Delegate. Trust. Depend. Engage. Facilitate. Develop. **Do all these things, and don't allow what you do to negatively impact WHO YOU ARE!** Success is always sweeter with true friends there to celebrate.

Notes:

_____

_____

_____

_____

_____

_____

_____

_____

 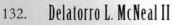

Rule #5

Lead LIFE OUT LOUD!

Pump up the volume!
Pump up the volume!
Pump up the volume!

LEAD! LEAD!

Listen, my friend. If you are really gonna do this college thing, you have to do it BIG and you have to do it LOUD! **Don't "half bake" your college leadership experience - do it BIG.** Since you are here, you might as well go all the way and give your everything! I want to challenge you to turn up the volume on your life, your personality, your presence, and your positive impact. **YOU SHOULD MASSIVELY IMPACT ANYTHING THAT YOU ARE A PART OF!** You should not do anything that is half-done. No...no...no! Whatever you commit to, you should GO ALL THE WAY with it. **Whatever you involve yourself in, do it to the very best of your ability and you will make an impact.** You should be such an asset to your organization that when you're gone – **people miss you.** Your presence, alone, should count for something significant. Whatever project you take on, you should impact it so much that people could easily tell that your fingerprints of greatness are ALL over it.

Autograph your work with excellence. Let excellence be your signature when it comes to functions, trips, conferences, meetings, assignments, and the whole nine.

Leadership Success

Turn up the volume on your life. Some people can't hear you right now! Your presence is not powerful enough. **Your positive attitude should be contagious. Your vocabulary should be uplifting and supportive. Your presence should be radiating excitement. Your ideas should be fresh, and your insight should be profound.** You are bad-to-the-bone, so make sure that you communicate to your campus how awesome you really and truly are. Be heard and make sure that you are respectful in the process, so that you will experience much success in leading out loud.

Notes:

_____

_____

_____

_____

_____

_____

_____

_____

Accept the Leadership Challenge

True leaders can lead during the good times and the bad. They lead when it is popular and when it is unpopular. They lead when everyone is on their side, and even when everyone seems to be talking about them behind their back. **Leaders understands that being well-liked by everyone is NOT high on their priority list.** In college, I had the wonderful opportunity to lead in a variety of settings, and overall, each one taught me lessons about leadership, life, and love.

As I have mentioned earlier in this book, I held several key leadership positions in college. Each one brought its own set of challenges and issues to the table. **The first, real one was when I decided to become an Orientation Leader (OL).** I loved that job and that leadership opportunity! I grew a lot, spoke a lot, met a lot of people, and impacted the lives of many students. I got a great deal of speaking opportunities from that position, but it had it's challenging times. There were times when we had to be back from holiday breaks early, times when we could not work outside jobs, and times when we had to sacrifice personal time to practice and rehearse for productions we wanted to put on for the students and their parents. Did I always like getting up at 6:00am every morning in the summer time? NOPE! However, I accepted the Leadership Challenge and I am now a better person and have a more successful business today because of what I learned as an OL at FSU.

My second, major challenge came when I became the 5th Floor Resident Assistant (RA) in a Private Housing Facility called Southgate. I really enjoyed our

Leadership Success

team of RAs and we worked very well together for the most part, but again, leadership has its challenges. I had free room and board, but students who were drunk repeatedly kept me up many nights monitoring the halls. I can remember stories about student life that would make your stomach turn, **but I endured the challenging times because I was willing to pay the price of comfort for the benefit of FREE room and board.**

The third, major challenge was when I was the President of the FSU Gospel Choir. Now, one of the things that determined the popularity of the choir was attendance at rehearsals. I remember being the president when we had 2 major choir director changes. The first one took the choir from 200 voices down to 40 voices - almost overnight. I mean, we dropped members so fast that it made my head spin. The students did not like the new style of music that the new director selected and taught, so the majority of them left. I remember for a solid year, it was not popular in Tallahassee to be considered a member of the FSU Gospel Choir. It wasn't because it was a bad organization, but because the songs that we were singing - were not "off the chain". We were singing older and more traditional sings, versus newer and more contemporary songs with cool beats. Well, that was a MAJOR leadership challenge for me because, on the one hand, I understood the concern of the students, but I also understood the direction of our leader and at that time they wanted us to do traditional music. After the first year, things did get better. The choir grew back in size, but it took both sides - the choir director and the students – meeting in the middle, negotiating, and compromising. It also took

A LOT OF PRAYER. Smiles!

I shared these three very brief examples with you just to teach you one powerful thing. **LEADERSHIP WILL CHALLENGE YOU!** It will not always be easy and it will not always be popular to be the leader of an organization. Sometimes, the most important function of a great leader is to SERVE someone else and to be an agent of positive change and progress within the organization. You've got what it takes to be a GREAT COLLEGIATE LEADER. In addition, you have what it takes to be a great leader in life - long after college is over. Simply, apply the principles that I and many other authors and speakers teach you, and you will "Write Your Own Ticket through Leadership – In College and Beyond!"

Notes:

_____

_____

_____

_____

_____

_____

_____

Leadership Success

_____

_____

_____

_____

_____

_____

_____

_____

_____

_____

_____

_____

_____

_____

_____

_____

_____

_____

_____

Chapter 11
Mentorship Success

Surround yourself with the 3 M's!

The moment that you begin to master this principle in your life, you will begin to take quantum leaps into your destiny. I believe that if you really want to grow rapidly and maintain a great degree of success in college and beyond, there are **3 types of individuals that you MUST surround yourself with.** Dr. Mike Murdock says, *"There are two ways to get wisdom - Mistakes and Mentors!"* I agree, wholeheartedly. That is why I want to teach you how to purposely put the right types of people in your life NOW, so that you will reap the benefits NOW & LATER.

The first person you need in your life is a MENTOR. This is someone who cuts your learning curve. A mentor is someone who exemplifies many qualities that you aspire towards in your life. You can have mentors in multiple areas of your life, but what I have found is that the best mentors are those who can teach you in a variety of different areas of life. Now, please understand what you are asking for when you ask for a mentor. You are asking for someone who is way ahead of you. You are asking for someone whose first priority in your life is NOT to be your friend. Rather, a mentor's #1 priority in your life is to be an agent of massive positive change in your life. **A mentor sees where you are in life, reaches down, and pulls you up to their level. Sometimes, a mentor even pushes you above levels that they themselves have yet to achieve.**

The second person you need in your life is a MATE. This is someone who walks alongside you and helps you make it through the day-to-day challenges and successes of

Mentorship Success

life. This person is like a running buddy. It is important that you pick the right types of people to be running buddies with because the LAST thing you want are people trying to slow you down. You want people with passion, energy, ambition, determination, and focus. **You want someone who is ON YOUR LEVEL.** This person is someone that you can study with, research with, go to conferences with, share successes with, and also grow and develop with. This is not necessarily a boyfriend or girlfriend. A mate is simply someone who is heading in the same general direction as you and the both of you realize that a partnership would be mutually beneficial.

The third person you need in your life is a MENTEE. A mentee is someone whose learning curve you cut. This is a person who looks at you just like you look at your mentor. Now, many people see the value of having a mentor, but it is much harder convincing people of the value of a mentee. Some people look at mentees as a waste of time and energy poured into someone who is lagging behind. Well, yes they are not where you are yet - but guess what? You are not where your mentor is yet either. So, make sure that you don't get "all high and mighty", just because you have a mentor and a mate. Don't forget to pour your life lessons into someone, such as a mentee, in your life. **A mentee forces you to learn from all your mistakes in life because they don't want to make the same ones that you did.** They also don't want to be a bother to your life. Therefore, you must make sure you treat them with care, because most mentees respect how busy you are and only want to learn from you, so keep that in mind. What does all this mean to YOU – the above average college student? Well, it means that there is someone who is younger than you - and even older than you - who could benefit greatly from your mentorship and leadership. There is someone, maybe in high school, who could avoid some major financial mistakes just by a few words of advice that you can share with them.

Regardless of where you are in your life while reading this chapter and regardless of how great you feel you are - you have the ability to PULL these 3 types of people into your life. You can create a master network of **people who will pull you, run with you, and pull from you, so that you can develop into the best YOU that you were born to be.**

Notes:

_____

_____

_____

_____

_____

_____

_____

Mentorship Success

Rule #2

Embrace and appreciate accountability!

One of the biggest functions of mentors is to help hold us accountable. Now, I know that the term "accountability" ranks high on your list of favorite words like budget, diet, and exams...Smiles. **However, accountability really is a very powerful principle that can help to shave years off of your development time.** Ultimately, this principle will keep you focused on doing the right things for the right reasons. When you think about accountability, make sure that you think in many other forms - not just people. For example, **your alarm clock** going off over and over again each morning is attempting to hold you accountable for getting up and out on time. **The watch you wear** does the same thing for you throughout your day. **Your cell phone** rings and many show an envelop on the display to hold you accountable for checking the messages that people leave you. In many vehicles, there is a **red light** coupled with a "dinging" sound that is trying to hold you accountable for putting on your seatbelt. **The microwave** "dings" when your food is ready to hold you accountable for getting it while it is hot.

All of these examples are real life scenarios of how we are constantly surrounded by things that were designed to hold us accountable. Think about how dangerous our highways are. Imagine how much more dangerous our highways would be if we did not **have speed limit signs, no passing zones, and police officers patrolling the roads.** All these measures are strategically put in place to hold all of us accountable for our actions.

Well, mentorship does the exact same thing for you in life. When you find the right mentors, be sure to understand that they really

Mentorship Success

and truly want the best for you. They are not trying to control your life, but they are trying to empower you and develop your life to a place that exemplifies absolute power, abundance, and greatness. So, when your mentor tells you that they don't recommend you buying a certain item that you really want, don't get mad. Get an understanding as to why they feel that way and work on dealing with it. I remember a time when I wanted to buy a new laptop (the one I am typing this book on right now). However, before I bought it, my mentor encouraged me not to. He reminded me that I still had debt on a credit card that I needed to pay off before I could purchase something new. He was right and he was holding my spending actions accountable for paying off debt first. I obeyed and paid off that debt, and within 1 week, I had the money I needed to get my new laptop. See my point? **There is safety and wisdom in accountability.**

Notes:

_____

_____

_____

_____

_____

_____

Focus on cutting your learning curve!

Learn how to ask better questions! Listen, when you get a mentor in life, one of your primary goals is to Duplicate their Success without **Duplicating all the Failure it took to get that Success in the first place.** Please understand something. **Just because you get mentors in your life does not - IN ANY WAY - exempt you from trouble.** No…No…No. In some instances, things get harder in your life when you get mentors because life won't just give up all the goods for nothing. It will cost you something, my friend. So, when living a life of mentorship, make sure that you are asking the right types of questions from your mentors. **Your goal is to create the same, if not better, results with less errors. THIS IS 100% POSSIBLE.** It's not using or taking advantage of people. It is being SMART. The person that does not learn from the mistakes of others is a FOOL. You are not a fool, so let's start cutting your learning curve. Now, there is a powerful statement that I must make that sets the stage for this rule.

Always pursue a mentor for what they have learned (i.e. wisdom, insight, and know-how) - not for what they have earned (i.e. degrees, cars, houses, diamond rings, etc.). When you ask questions of people, you must ask destiny questions what will give you destiny answers. Don't ask "Where did you buy that brand new Mercedes Benz you drive?" That is a wasted question. Rather, ask *"How did you set yourself up financially to buy that vehicle with CASH. Also, how did you negotiate the dealer down from the sticker price?"* Now you are asking questions that will teach you the way your mentor THINKS. **Stop pursuing the THINGS of your mentor and start pursuing the THOUGHTS**

Mentorship Success

of your mentor. If you can learn why successful people think WHAT they think, then you are 50% of the way there. Rich people think differently from poor people. Successful people think different thoughts than unsuccessful people do.

Ask questions that start with WHY and HOW instead of WHAT and ARE. For example, when you meet with someone who is financially successful, don't ask, "Are you a millionaire?" Instead ask, "How did you become a millionaire?" This becomes a totally different question simply by changing one word. Learn how to ask better questions because **the better the questions, the more years you can cut from your learning curve and get results quicker.**

Notes:

_____

_____

_____

_____

_____

_____

_____

Rule #4

Network with people of positive influence!

Be where people of influence are...PERIOD! Be in the right place at the right time. So what if you don't know exactly what you want to be in life yet? So what if you don't know how you are going to afford the rest of your education? So what if you can't seem to find someone to really love you like you want to be loved? So what if clubs and organizations don't seem to offer exactly what you want to get involved with? **Put your personal issues aside and push yourself to get around Powerful and Positive People.** God knows, there are enough negative people in this world. You must seek out the positive ones, but please remember one thing. There are plenty of great people out there.

- **People of positive influence** can see things in you that you don't see in yourself. They can help you get a vision of your tomorrow, even when your today seems a little cloudy.
- **People of positive influence** will never be satisfied with leaving you where you are right now. They will challenge you to become greater than you are.
- **People of positive influence** will help to open doors for you that you would not be able to open for yourself. If you were able to open those doors, it would take you much longer.
- **People of positive influence** can tell when you are feeding them a bunch of excuses and non-sense. They can also tell when you are giving your absolute best in what you do.

Mentorship Success

- **People of positive influence** hang around people of positive influence - so to find them. Look for people of positive influence.
- **People of positive influence** have a very low tolerance for mediocrity, drama, gossip, strife, and negativity. They simply are too busy and too focused to entertain foolishness, so don't come to them with it and don't try to involve them in it either.
- **People of positive influence** are not perfect people. They are not God. They are not to be worshipped or put on pedestals. Rather, they are to be supported and appreciated - not idolized.

As you can see, there is tremendous value to be found in networking and associating yourself with people who are going somewhere positive in life. My challenge to you is to find these people, and in the process, BECOME one of these types of persons as well. You can and must do it!

Notes:

_____

_____

_____

_____

_____

Interview yourself & your mentor!

The following are **5 questions you should ask yourself BEFORE** you approach someone to be a mentor in your life.

1. Am I ready **to be challenged, stretched, and developed?**
2. Am I willing to **put my own agenda to the side** and work with my mentor to create an agenda that helps develop me faster?
3. Am I willing to **push my pride and my ego to the side** and humble myself to be guided and directed by someone who knows a lot more than I do in this particular area of life?
4. Am I willing to **work for GREATNESS?** I'm not planning to work for nothing, but if I don't get a penny, will I still know that I am more than satisfied working with this person to obtain purpose and power in my life?
5. Am I **excited about my own growth?** Am I willing to contribute to the overall betterment of my mentor and their vision?

The following are **5 questions you should ask the person you would like to mentor you.** You can have this dialogue over a lunch that YOU pay for, or in their office at a time that is convenient for THEM.

1. I am very interested in being mentored by you. **Are you currently in a position to mentor someone** with the gifts, talents, and destiny that I possess?

Mentorship Success

Delatorro L. McNeal II 151.

2. I am not coming to this mentorship relationship empty-handed. May I please briefly share with you some skills that **I believe will make me a true asset** to your vision, both personally and professionally?

3. I see greatness in my future, but I trust that you probably see more for me than maybe I see for myself. This being so, **will you share with me what you see in my future?**

4. **What are my blind spots?** What are the areas of my life that need development, that I may be a little naive to.

5. When is the **best time for us to communicate? How regular would you like me to contact you? Which form of communication is best for you** (i.e., email, office, cell phone, hand-written letters, etc.)?

6. **What tasks, assignments, or projects** may I begin working on with you so that I can begin to show you, first hand, the asset I can be to this relationship?

Ask these questions of yourself and your mentors and you will be well on your way to creating and sustaining powerful mentorship relationships that will help you to *Write Your Own Ticket, In College & Beyond!*

Notes: _____

_____

_____

_____

Chapter 12

Entrepreneurship
& Career Success

Rule #1

Write your own ticket!

Congratulations! You have made it to the final chapter of this great book and I am very proud of you. This rule is very special because it represents the core theme of the entire book. My friend, I want you to know how special and dynamic you really are. **You are a wonderful human being with gifts, talents, abilities, ideas, and skills that this world NEEDS.** Please understand that you have the power to WRITE YOUR OWN TICKET if you choose. You see, you can come to college, graduate, and work for someone else all of your life, and that is fine. That would just mean that you wrote your ticket to work for someone else all your life – and if you are happy doing that, then GREAT. However, you also have the power to come to college, graduate, work for someone else to gain experience, and then ultimately work for yourself and have people work for YOU. **Now, THAT INDEED is what I call WRITING YOUR OWN TICKET.** 90% of employees in today's job market want more money. Working for someone else will never bring you the kind of income you want. Why? It is because THEY are writing the ticket for you. They are labeling you and telling you what you are worth, rather than you telling the world what you are worth and making the world react to your marketing. There is nothing at all wrong with working for a great organization. I highly recommend it. However, there is something extremely wrong with hating what you do all of your life and sentencing yourself to low salaries, low standards of living, low family happiness, and low confidence.

When you work for others, you must always measure up to their standards and do things their way. **When you work for yourself, YOU set the bar for yourself.** Also, you get a new opportunity to raise the bar and better your best everyday! **College is a very special and monumental time in your life. You will make decisions in college that can either set you up for tremendous success or sentence you to tremendous failure.** The concept of "Writing Your Own Ticket" means that you don't wait for life to hand you anything. You go after what you desire and honestly believe that you can achieve it. The collegiate experience gives you many of the tools that you'll need while working for others and for yourself. Ultimately, it is your call. You must decide to be happy in life based on YOU! Remember that your life and the happiness and true contentment that you want in life, is a direct result of the decisions and choices you make. Choose wisely and choose powerfully.

Notes:

_____

_____

_____

_____

_____

_____

_____

_____

Rule #2

Operate as the CEO of your own life!

The Chief Executive Officer (CEO) is not just the top-dog of a major corporation. **The CEO is you!** You are the CEO of your own life. You are the top-dog, and YOU are the head person in charge of either making your life great or making it miserable. **Don't give away the tremendous amount of power that you possess by not being the CEO of your life.** Take control and take charge of your life, your career, your college experience, and your destiny. Take control of your relationships, your time, your talents, and your future. **Get out of the comfortable seats of coach class, and get into the pilot seat on the flight that is destined for your future.** If you don't, you will land in destinations that you never intended to. Now please understand, I am not encouraging you to be bossy, snooty, or cocky. **In fact, I want you to be the exact opposite of that and STILL be the CEO of your life.** When you get your own business one day, you will be the CEO of that organization. However, until that time comes, you are still a CEO...the CEO OF YOU! In fact, that will never change. **Successful entrepreneurs are CEOs in their minds LONG before they are CEOs on paper.**

A CEO understands several paradigms about life that make them very successful in mind, body, spirit, business, relationships, and the marketplace. My challenge to you is to embrace these beliefs and implement them into your DNA (Daily Natural Action).

First, CEOs understand that choices and decisions shape destiny. Wishing it and wanting it does nothing. For

Entrepreneurship & Career Success

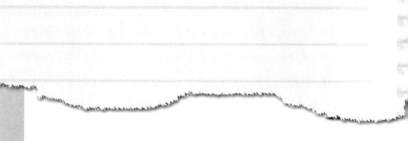

greatness to be born, it will require the midwife of action to be taken towards purpose-driven decisions.

Second, CEOs understand that the world owes them nothing. Everything they acquire, they expect it from themselves and life must yield it. They do believe that good things come to those who wait, but only the things left by those who hustle. They get started and keep moving forward.

Third, CEOs understand the importance of an executive board. They are a group of like-minded people in their lives that can shape and empower their destiny. They know that their life only becomes better when they, themselves, become better. CEOs understand that they are life-long learners. They understand that learning more, equates to earning more. They are proactive!

Fourth, the Collegiate CEO understands the difference between facts and truth. They know that facts are actual accounts of things that took place, but they also know that truth is the revelation of what a person, place, or thing really is and can be. I'll give you an example. **Fact:** you got a C- this semester in a course you thought you could Ace. Well, the fact may be that you got a below average grade, but the **truth** is that you are a blossoming A+ student who is simply overcoming some academic challenges right now. Do you see my point? Allow me to give you another example. **Fact:** your date treats you like crap and makes you feel like you are worth nothing and that no one will ever treat you better. Well my friend, that may be an actual account of what happened. However, that is not truth. The **truth** is

Delatorro L. McNeal II

that you are a radiant, brilliant, and unique human being who deserves the best companion that life has to offer. The truth is that, as soon as you drop that zero in your life and prove to yourself that you don't need to hang with turkeys in order to soar like an eagle, you will attract into your life the person that has been divinely assigned to bless your life.

So, the CEO understands these and many other powerful realities about life that will make her/him massively successful - both in college and beyond. Make sure that you, as the CEO of your life, understand them and implement them as well.

Notes:

_____

_____

_____

_____

_____

_____

_____

_____

_____

Entrepreneurship & Career Success

Notes:

_____

_____

_____

_____

_____

_____

_____

_____

_____

_____

_____

_____

_____

_____

_____

_____

_____

Rule #3

Extract life application nuggets from each class!

The CEO of the College Experience walks into each classroom and looks at the entire environment as a life teacher. Not just the instructor, but also the students, the atmosphere, the culture, and the dynamics of the course communicate to the Collegiate CEO (YOU) that there is much to learn besides the facts in the book. **In order to be a CEO internally - long before you experience it externally, you must begin to ask yourself questions during the course of your semester that will give you profound answers that will help you to act and produce results in your life.** Start thinking like an entrepreneur! Ask yourself these questions and see what answers you come up with.

1. How does this course play into the BIG PICTURE of my Collegiate Development?

2. What qualities or characteristics about the instructor do I like that I should implement into my personal style?

3. What qualities or characteristics about the instructor do I dislike that I should avoid implementing into my personal style?

4. How could I ultimately use this information in my business?

5. What examples from real life can I parallel with this learning material to make it more relevant to me?

Entrepreneurship & Career Success

Delatorro L. McNeal II   161.

Trust me, my friend. The purpose of certain classes I took in college was not clear to me while I was in there. However, **now I can appreciate 95% of the courses I took. The knowledge I gained from each course came back to play a role - regardless of how small - in my future!** There will be many classes that are boring, hard, and down-right pointless. Regardless, you must keep in mind that your future will hand you situations to walk through that are similar to what you learned in those classes. So, just look at those courses as teaching you stamina, persistence, and determination to get through the things you don't enjoy. **Remember, if you are willing to do what you HAVE to do, the day will soon come when you will GET to do what you WANT to do!**

Notes:

_____

_____

_____

_____

_____

_____

_____

Rule #4

Know yourself!

In order to be a successful entrepreneur, you MUST know yourself. Know your **likes and your dislikes.** Know why you do many of the things that you do. Know your **values and your beliefs.** Know **what you stand for and what you stand against.** Know your **gifts and your talents.** Know your **strengths and weaknesses.** In college, we place so much emphasis on knowing a lot about many different subjects, about our major, about our clubs and organizations, and about our future field of specialization. **What I have found is that many people who enter college, go through college, and exit college, never really know about THEMSELVES.** It is so very important that you know **yourself,** know your **life story,** and know your **experiences.** If YOU don't, you can't expect others to either.

I have had the wonderful opportunity of being on both sides of the interview table. I was interviewed a lot in college. However, in grad school and after college, I did and still do a great amount of interviewing. As the interviewer, I have found one major flaw in most of the people I've interviewed. **Although they know about the company, their major, and even a little about the person who is interviewing them – most people don't know about themselves.** They get stumped on questions about personal stories from their past, plans for their future, and experiences in their present that are relevant to a business environment. Oh, and many people lie too. So remember to not say things in an interview that are not consistent with your resume. Why? Because Human Resources (HR) specialists do reference checks and past employment verifications to see if you lied about something. For example, they may check to see if you lied about something

Entrepreneurship & Career Success

small, such as how long you worked at McDonalds 5 years ago. If they catch you in a lie, they automatically toss your application because they feel that you will lie about bigger things as well. **Remember, your only competition when going for jobs, internships, and other career opportunities is YOURSELF.** Don't try to be better than anyone else. Just be the best that YOU can be. In doing so, you will rise above the so-called "competition".

Another tip about success in jobs and careers is to **learn the buzzwords that get you in the door of the field of your interest**. Salt and pepper your resume and cover letter with words and phrases that **mean something significant** to the people in that industry. **Expand your vocabulary to include verbiage that makes you seem well-versed and well-read within your chosen field of interest.** I know people who got picked for interviews and interest meetings simply because they knew how to use the right words to attract the right attention to their resume. **Listen, your resume has to speak volumes about you in your ABSENCE.** It has to stand on its own two feet and represent you. Presentation is very important, so invest in resume writing workshops, books, and other materials that will help you get the edge you need to be very successful. **Remember, you must know yourself and TELL THE WORLD how BAD you are!**

Rule #5

Master the Interview Process!

There are plenty of great books out there that will teach you how to interview successfully. Get those books and implement what they teach. In this rule, **I just want to share with you, from PERSONAL EXPERIENCE, some techniques that I have used and seen used that have guaranteed great success in interviews.** Activate these ideas into your interviews and watch the great results you'll get.

1. Before the interview, **research the website and financial materials about the organization.** Ask your roommate or friend to quiz you on the "quick facts" about the organization. **Don't ask for a job if you are not willing to learn about the organization in advance.**

2. Before the interview, research the interview location, know about traffic, know the exact location, and plan to arrive at least 1 hour early.

3. Before the interview, **prepare a list of questions that YOU will ask after you've been interviewed.** Doing this shows that you are proactive and have a sincere passion to make sure that the organization is a good match for you and vice versa.

4. Before the interview, **dress above the culture of the organization for the sake of the first impression.** Remember a few essentials: breath mints, a nice portfolio folder with paper and extra resumes, a nice writing pen, Chap Stick if needed, and turn your cell phone OFF.

Entrepreneurship & Career Success

5. During the interview, sit erect, yet comfortable. Please don't talk or posture yourself like a robot. Be yourself and **be powerful in your presence.** Avoid fidgeting with your hair and nails, tapping your feet, and other signs of nervousness.

6. **During the interview, make sure that you answer the questions that are asked. Don't go off on tangents of information that the interviewer never asked for.** Be direct, polite, succinct, and clear.

7. During the interview, admit when you don't know the answer to a question that they ask. **Don't make up stuff - just be honest.** Smile often and smile genuinely. Create a flow in the conversation and be a nice person to talk to - not just to interview.

8. During the interview, **ask "non-threatening" questions about the interviewer's personal passion behind his or her decision to work for the organization. Ask for a "Day in the Life" example.**

9. After the interview, **ask your questions and take notes when they are answered.** This lets the interviewer know that you really care about retaining the information that is shared with you.

10. After the interview, ask the **MILLION DOLLAR QUESTION.** Wanna know what that question is? Here it goes! Ask the interviewer, **"If you were me, what other questions would you ask someone like yourself, who**

has succeeded at your level in the organization?" This question is POWERFUL and it gets the interviewer on your side immediately. This question shows that you value what they have learned and it shows that you are big into learning fast!

11. After the interview, stand at the appropriate time, **present your business card** (Don't have one? Get one at www.vistaprint.com.), and give a pleasant and firm handshake with direct eye contact.

12. After the interview, **send a hand written personal thank you card, and an email to the interviewer.** In your note and email, thank them for their time, conversation, and the wealth of information they shared with you.

My friend, if you will study these two pages of techniques for mastering the interviewing process and implement the many other skills that you have developed and learned along the way, you will be in great shape to do very well with your interviews and, as a result, career opportunities. Best wishes and God Bless!

Notes:

_____

_____

_____

_____

_____

_____

_____

_____

_____

_____

_____

_____

_____

_____

_____

_____

_____

_____

_____

_____

_____

_____

Rule #6

Make College Count, then MOVE ON!

After everything I have taught you, advised you, coached you, and showed you in this book, I want to leave you with one final rule. **Make this thing called college really count for something big in your life.** Many people look back on their college days with regret because they did not pursue their dream while they had a chance. They did not create the type of life they wanted while they had the energy to do so. They did not pick a major that meant something special to THEM. They did not maintain healthy bodies, healthy habits, and healthy relationships.

DON'T LET THIS BE YOU.
DON'T GET CAUGHT IN THAT TRAP!

Make your collegiate years significantly count towards building your future, apprehending your greatness, and pursuing your destiny. Part of college is searching, but **more of college involves discovering.** Part of college is struggling, but **more of college involves succeeding.** Part of college is confusion and frustration, but **more of college involves decisions and intelligent action.** Part of college is bad attitudes, but **more of college involves great, life-long relationships.** So...

DON'T ALLOW the PARTS to DEVALUE the MORE & the WHOLE!

There is a HUGE world and a great life that awaits you upon graduation and the completion of your college experience. Realize that. There are more

Entrepreneurship & Career Success

people for you to meet, more relationships to establish, more territory to discover, and more opportunity to create and seize after college. Realize that. **There is a divine soul mate out there waiting to discover you. Don't settle for 2nd best, but don't under-appreciate a good thing either.** What you like, someone else hates. What you think is trash, someone else thinks is a treasure. One man's floor is another man's ceiling. **Realize that.**

They call your official graduation from college a "Commencement Ceremony" for a very empowering reason. Commencement does not mean "the end"; instead, it means **"THE BEGINNING"**. The start of something new, awesome, powerful, blessed, deserved, and destined! Congratulations in advance, my dear friend. Apply these rules and you will, indeed, be able to…

WRITE YOUR OWN TICKET, IN COLLEGE and BEYOND!